GUY ANDREWS and ROHAN DUBASH
with photography by TAZ DARLING

BIKE MECHANIC
TALES FROM THE ROAD AND THE WORKSHOP

BLOOMSBURY

The inspiration for us following mechanics and team trucks around the world was a book called Bicycle Mechanics in Workshop and Competition by Steve Snowling and Ken Evans. Published in 1985, it was the bible for budding bike mechanics like Rohan Dubash and myself. I first met Rohan a decade or so later at Cycles Dauphin on top of Box Hill in Surrey where we shared some workshop time together. We used to play a game, each day we'd take it in turns to bring a different part from a bicycle component into the workshop; a spring, a bolt, a plastic shim or an unusual washer. We'd try to catch one another out. I'm sure I was left scratching my head on many occasions, but fooling Rohan was impossible — he's forgotten more about bicycles than most of us know. So, this book is a collection of stories with some tips and hints that we thought would be useful to amateur mechanics and road cycling enthusiasts alike. It certainly isn't comprehensive, there just wasn't space, but if this proves popular, a second edition will no doubt follow.

We hope it inspires you to get the workstand out.

GUY ANDREWS

Published by Rouleur Books
An imprint of Bloomsbury
Publishing Plc
50 Bedford Square
London WC1B 3DP
www.bloomsbury.com

First edition 2014

**Editor: Guy Andrews
Copy editor: Claire Read
Designer: Rob Johnston
Assistant designer: Chris Martin
All photography © Taz Darling
and Guy Andrews**

Made from wood grown in managed, sustainable forests. It is natural, renewable and recyclable. The logging and manufacturing processes conform to the environmental regulations of the country of origin.

Printed and bound in China by C&C Offset Printing Ltd

10 9 8 7 6 5 4 3 2 1

Gruppo Media Limited
10th Floor Holborn Tower
137 High Holborn
London WC1V 6PW
www.rouleur.cc

Rouleur magazine is published eight times a year
ISSN 1752–962X

This book is dedicated to Ned 1939–2013.
He always said that if you looked after your tools, they would look after you...

ON THE ROAD

LE MÉTIER

THE DAILY GRIND
LA RUTINA DIARIA
DAS TÄGLICHE SCHLEIFEN

Long days and longer nights

One pair of hands is all that is needed and the best respected mechanics are the ones who take charge of a situation and have a calm and considered approach.

Post-crash, the race is chaotic and confusing for the mechanics. Finding your rider is one thing. Finding their bike can be even more of a challenge.

There was a time when adjusting a bike needed a lot of tools — even setting up a pair of brakes required hours of patience. In the days before lucrative sponsorship deals and huge annual budgets, bike teams had to seek mechanics out as contractors. They were often hired hands from the bike stores and workshops of a team's native country; sometimes ex-racers or framebuilders or bicycle factory workers who got an annual summer sabbatical to follow their dreams and their heroes. With their tools, they would head off to the Tour de France or the Giro d'Italia. It sounds great, and romantic. But it's hard work and the ultimate aim was always the same — to keep the guys on the road.

Good team mechanics can make a massive difference to the outcome of a race. Today, pros expect a perfectly prepared bike and a host of high-tech solutions to make it comfortable and efficient. But the art of fixing bikes was once a much more mysterious talent. For example, prior to the 1955 Giro d'Italia, Fiorenzo Magni was frustrated and struggling with knee problems. Somewhat ambitiously a young Ernesto Colnago persuaded Magni to let him have the bike in for repair. Colnago had spotted that Magni's cranks were misaligned and running unevenly. He knew immediately that the cotter pins holding the chainset to the axle had to be accurately re-filed for the crank arms to line up perfectly, and he worked hard to perfect the crooked drivetrain. His attention to detail was admirable. Magni's knees recovered; Colnago was established.

This type of repair was not unusual in the 1950s. Racing bikes of the era required a lot of fettling and good mechanics like Colnago were highly regarded. Wheels needed constant truing, brakes had to be set up on a daily basis and gears were constantly on the point of breaking down. Ask any current team mechanic about the tools of their trade and they will say that they only need a handful of simple ones to keep a modern racing bike on the road. In fact, most days, the bikes just need a wash and some fresh bar tape — serious problems are rare. In Colnago's day, you needed a watchmaker's attention to detail and an engineer's workshop to carry out even the most basic repair, so very few mechanics could cut it on the demanding professional circuit.

Colnago's repairs quickly built him a formidable reputation both in the workshop and at the races. His apprenticeship as a welder at Italian racing bike giant Gloria meant he could build frames too. Soon many top stars were calling on his services, even those with other bike sponsors. He always worked hard, often staying up all night in his tiny workshop — once to build more than 10 pairs of wheels for a local team the night before a stage race. But Ernesto was more than just a grafter. He had a sickness, an addiction. His creativity and engineering talent meant that his 'Wizard' nickname was soon established and his pride in his work rewarded.

Mechanical talent from the four corners of the world

Tales of how the big names in cycling started out as mechanics are not unusual. Reputations are built from the ground up and the best technicians, bike designers and framebuilders have to work hard to break into the world of professional mechanic. Today Yoshiaki Nagasawa is one of the most sought after framebuilders in the world. But in the 1970s he had to travel to Italy and to professional racing to learn his trade.

"I started when I was at De Rosa. No wait, I had one year with Sante Pogliaghi in Italy, but I was a mechanic. I didn't go there to learn to build frames, but actually learn to prepare bikes for racers. I mean at the Giro d'Italia, these mechanics will prepare 10 bikes overnight. I had to see how that is done.

"That is what I did at De Rosa, too — preparing bikes for Eddy Merckx and Gianni Motta. But to be able to assemble bikes for them properly, I needed to understand all the geometries and construction of the frame itself. As for the method of building, I just watched the old man [Ugo De Rosa] build frames every day.

Soigneurs with spare wheels are spread all over a race's *parcours*. Extreme events with demanding conditions like Paris-Roubaix can mean up to 20 extra mechanics and team helpers out on the course.

"I went to Italy in 1970, so I'm not sure when I actually started building frames as opposed to being a mechanic, but probably 1972 or '73. I came back to Japan in '76 and started building frames as a profession. The presidents of Sugino and Nitto were in Milan every year and they took care of me when I was starting out.

"I knew that it would be impossible to make a living being a mechanic, but I knew that I could do it by becoming a framebuilder for keirin racers. There were lot of road bike builders, but there were only a few track frame builders then. I was number 170 of the registered keirin builders, but many were gone. I was the first to put my own name on the down tube, which is normal in Italy, but in Japan they all come up with these silly brand names. De Rosa didn't do any track frames, but Pogliaghi did, so I referred to their experience.

"Of course, the way De Rosa did the frames has the most influence. Geometry-wise, Pogliaghi track bikes. The lug shapes and finishing is all from De Rosa.

"If I had to prepare frames for Eddy Merckx, I made sure it was superbly done — even Ugo couldn't match it. I made absolutely sure I left no room for Ugo to come in and retouch my work — I was proud of that. I did have Masi's finishing in my mind, but I was aiming to surpass them. Masi's frame back then was amazingly beautiful. But by the time I left Italy, I was better. I knew that.

"I think one of the coolest races to be at is the Tour of Flanders, or Paris-Roubaix because of all the things with the bikes — the wheels, tubulars and all of the kit and just to see all the fans trying to see their idols when they are riding the biggest one day races on the calendar."

RUNE KRISTENSEN

At the trucks before a time trial start the riders' turbo trainers are all laid out. The mechanics will change the rider's race wheels for a training pair for the warm up. Then it's back to the best pair for the race itself.

"Italy was crazy. Constantly hiding from the police, working late nights as I could have been deported any day — I had to work 150 per cent at all times. I did one day's worth of work in six hours. If I was done with one thing, I demanded them to give me more work. If still no work, then I cleaned up the shop, toilets — anything to help Ugo.

"One day, he came up to me and whispered: 'We are rich'. I mean, there were only two of us, and we were making 50 frames every month — 30 to 40 were complete bikes. I did everything myself, including packing and shipping [to Japan], building bikes for pros. Ugo never did anything beside weld frames. His wife did the bar tapes. She was good with wrapping and picky. She could wrap five bikes with four sets of bar tapes. She was clever, not wasteful!

"Today, designs are done on a computer, but the problem is the frame itself never comes out exactly the same when you start making it. Software is only smart up to pre-assembly before putting the torch on it. From there it's all experience — I can't calculate it. That's why I can't use standard jigs. I have my own jigs for my own methods."

When steel and aluminium were still popular choices, it made sense to custom build for most if not all riders. Carbon fibre frames, with their moulds and complicated tube patterns, make custom build a tricky and expensive business. Even so, custom built carbon frames are more prevalent than you

Improvising on the road is the job of the mechanic. They have to be fast, resourceful and highly skilled. Each day is a combination of adventure, problem solving and dogged determination to get the job done. Every day is different— it's a bit like a military operation.

would imagine among the more particular riders of the peloton. You have to be pretty eagle-eyed to spot them, though.

Dario Pegoretti was one of those frame-builders who developed techniques and fits for riders who wanted lighter bikes than the stock frame they had been offered.

"I was very lucky because in my work a big [part of my] experience was with a young team. I was working very, very closely with a young team called Riboli who were based in Ilasi. From 1980 to '85 it was one of the most important young teams in Italy; Davide Rebellin rode for the team when he was young. This was a good experience because I was free. It was a different experience—different to a pro team who always supply you with a chart

and you just build the frames, sometimes there is a top pro rider who comes to the shop and asks for an opinion, but normally not, [batch building] is not a stupid job, but it's not very exciting.

"But this job, with 20 riders, I started in January and every year or two it changes. I remember in two months I'd build 20 frames. It is very exciting [when] the guys take the bike and ride the bike. I remember I'd take the scooter. To ride with them as they trained— to have an opinion. This was very important and I think this was a great experience.

"I made more than 200 frames for them from 1991 to 1996. I made some mistakes here because I think it is impossible not to. Nowadays you take five different [statistical] systems

Team helpers always wear their team's jersey or a gilet, but it's usually a long sleeve training top. They're always easy to pick out at the Tour of Flanders because no Belgian would dream of wearing a team jersey to go and watch a bike race.

and five different guys you have five different results. It's impossible — you can have an idea with numbers but you can't get it right. But it is a question of experience, you know, and when you make a mistake, you can understand many more things from a mistake. I can't say that every one was perfect, but I can change it. Take a frame and build the whole frame and another frame and then compare.

"I build a frame, for the mechanics the bike's ready in two days. Meet all the guys and I take the car or a scooter and ride alongside of the guys and 'see' the mistakes. Write some notes. Come back to the shop on Monday and by two weeks build another frame. And you can compare the two frames, and see why you made a mistake..."

Mistakes can be hard to come to terms with but, in fairness, in the world of professional mechanics they are pretty rare. Out on the road with Kris Withington from Garmin, I asked him what the riders gave him the hardest time about.

"They don't. We put the pressure on ourselves and feel it ourselves. I don't think the riders complain much, they don't come down here and rip into us directly, but if something goes wrong with the bike, it's hard. Especially for GC riders like Millar or Christian Vande Velde or last year [2009] Bradley Wiggins.

"Wiggins is pretty cool about it all, but when you hear them on race radio screaming: 'My fucking bike, my fucking bike, my fucking bike!' it's bad for us, sure, but they don't come

Very often the mechanic is the one who has to push a stricken rider back into the race. Team managers will only usually get out of the car if they absolutely have to.

down to the truck and rip into us personally. The worst thing is, after a race where something goes wrong, the director comes and says: 'Hey, what happened there?' Normally the directors straight away support us and they look at the facts first, but if it's our fault, it's tough. But hey, that's the difference between a mechanic's job and a *soigneur's* job. A mechanic's job, if you fuck it up, it can actually cost the race. A *soigneur* can't really fuck up. I mean, how do you fuck up a massage? And even if you do mess it up somehow, it isn't going to cost them the race. But cycling's on TV and if something happens, it looks bad for us.

"Like David Millar's chain snapping in the Vuelta, that wasn't very pleasant, although that wasn't our fault. He was in the break all

day, and I was feeding him water and Coke all day out of the car, and then five kilometres from the line the chain started ticking, but he didn't bother to change the bike. We had a bike ready but he thought he'd be alright. And then when they started the sprint, he was going to win the stage easy, then the chain went — bang! And you could see on TV, he chucked the bike — fwoom! And because I was in the second car that day, we were already stuck in the deviation behind the race traffic, so I couldn't get to Dave to get him his spare bike — so he was just left standing there. Then the other mechanic had to run, and at that stage we were back in the convoy — so he had to run up with someone else's bike, for him just to cross the finish line. So that was a

Muddy and dusty races mean a load more work for the mechanic.

bad day, worse was we didn't know what the problem was. We thought: 'What the fuck's going on here?' So we changed, basically we put a new gruppo on his bike, and Shimano in Japan investigated.

"Finally, it turned out that there had been a bad run of chains. Every Shimano chain has a code on them so they could check. At the time, though, they thought it was something we'd done, but it wasn't. We finished work and were at the hotel, and David was sitting at the bar and said to me: 'Hey Kris, come on'—and we had four beers."

Team Saxo-Tinkoff mechanic Rune Kristensen had a similarly frustrating experience at the 2010 Tour de France, when one of his charges was in the yellow jersey.

"My worst experience was in the Tour 2010 when Andy Schleck lost his chain. We could not do anything—just sit and watch it on the TV in the car. I was in the second car that day. He lost his chain from the big chainring and couldn't get it back on again, it got trapped and it took ages to get it back on again. We checked the bike so many times after that day, but we never found what was wrong."

As bikes have changed so has the mechanic's job, mainly because the components are so much better than they were. Even so, the team mechanics are—without doubt—the busiest personnel on the team. They still love a chat, though, and so I asked Kris Withington how he'd wound up in this line of work.

Storing the bikes at night is another responsibility that the mechanics take very seriously. Team trucks are now targets for thieves, so usually all the kit — bikes, wheels, spares and toolkits — needs to be taken into the hotel each night. Here the laundry becomes an impromptu service course.

"I just I gave them my CV, but in this job a CV doesn't mean shit, really, does it? And then a month later, I got an email — here's your contract, see you in November for the training camp. I was really lucky, because on the team in 2008, everyone was basically a young neo pro, so I got to do everything. It wasn't like the older staff get preference or anything, so in my first year I got to do all the big races — the Giro and the Tour and all the Classics.

"That first year we were all just finding our way, and then the next year we thought: 'Oh, that didn't work so well last year', and so on. We had some cock ups in year one, but more or less from the riders' point of view we were fine. It's not like we were running around, going: 'Oh, we don't know what to do!' We knew what

to do, more or less — we didn't cost them the race or anything...

"The thought of that sometimes keep you awake at night, especially if you're on the verge of winning a race, like we were on the verge of winning the Three Days of De Panne in 2009 with David Millar. First thing in the morning I'd be down at the truck checking what we had done the night before...

"In 2008 at Paris-Roubaix, none of the team had done it before, so we just thought the preparation we were doing was correct. Because we didn't do Gent-Wevelgem that year, we had five days in between Flanders and Paris-Roubaix to get set. And even the night before we were out at the truck until 8pm, running around. We arrived at the start

Holding on to the team car at 70km/h while someone leans over you and frees a plastic bag from your gears isn't a job for the faint of heart.

and half the tubulars were wrong on top of the car — and different bikes everywhere. We had Magnus Backstedt riding a normal pair of carbon deep-section wheels, and then as soon as he got to Arenberg Forest, boom! We lost our team captain. But then the crazy thing was that everyone thought we were fine — Martijn Maaskant was fourth. So it was fine, you know [even though] we had the team leader break both of his wheels as soon as he got on to the forest. It was his decision to ride the wheels, but if we had had some more experience, we'd have said, "Hey — use these!"

"When we race, that's good. We're here at Paris-Roubaix — biggest race of the year, preparing the bikes for some big riders, potential

winners. That's good. Normally when you're on a race, there's always something good to do, especially the Classics because they're just so exceptional, and Paris-Roubaix even more so.

"These days in between, say, Scheldeprijs and Paris-Roubaix, it takes a lot of work to get these bikes good and strong. And then you've got Flanders and Paris-Roubaix bikes spare as well, and that's a lot of work to get those all exactly the same, do exactly the same things to three bikes. So if you build the race bike and then do the same thing three times over, four times over, that'll be a whole day's work, probably, building those bikes, preparing those spare bikes. Because they'll be out training and the bikes are out of the

Puncturing can be very stressful for a rider, so a mechanic needs to be able to reassure them by being in control. These days, practising wheel and bike changes is all part of the modern day marginal gains approach to the sport.

truck pretty much all day, every day, for the Classics. We get breakfast at 8am, so we're out here about 8.30am—and we usually have dinner at 8pm, so we try to finish at 7pm. Every day, whatever.

"Last year was good for the mechanics. We worked really well, had no problems the whole Tour. Of course, these are the two biggest Grand Tours, but the Tour de France is much easier than the Giro for us, because the hotels are usually just off the motorway. It's just routine—a rider might crash or you need to change a gear lever, and that's a novelty, really. And the rest days are a real pain in the arse, because you're full gas and it's busy at the truck with the media all around, and you have to change all the chains, clean all the

bikes—the rest days are the worst days in the whole Tour.

"But it's the Tour de France—everyone's hyped up for the whole time. And the riders change as the race goes on, because they get more and more tired which places a strain on team morale. In the Giro, we were all fired up for the first week, and then the rest of the race the boys were using it as training for the Tour. So it was like full gas—the stress was here for the first week and the days before the team time trial, and then Tyler Farrar winning. After that it was a lot more relaxed."

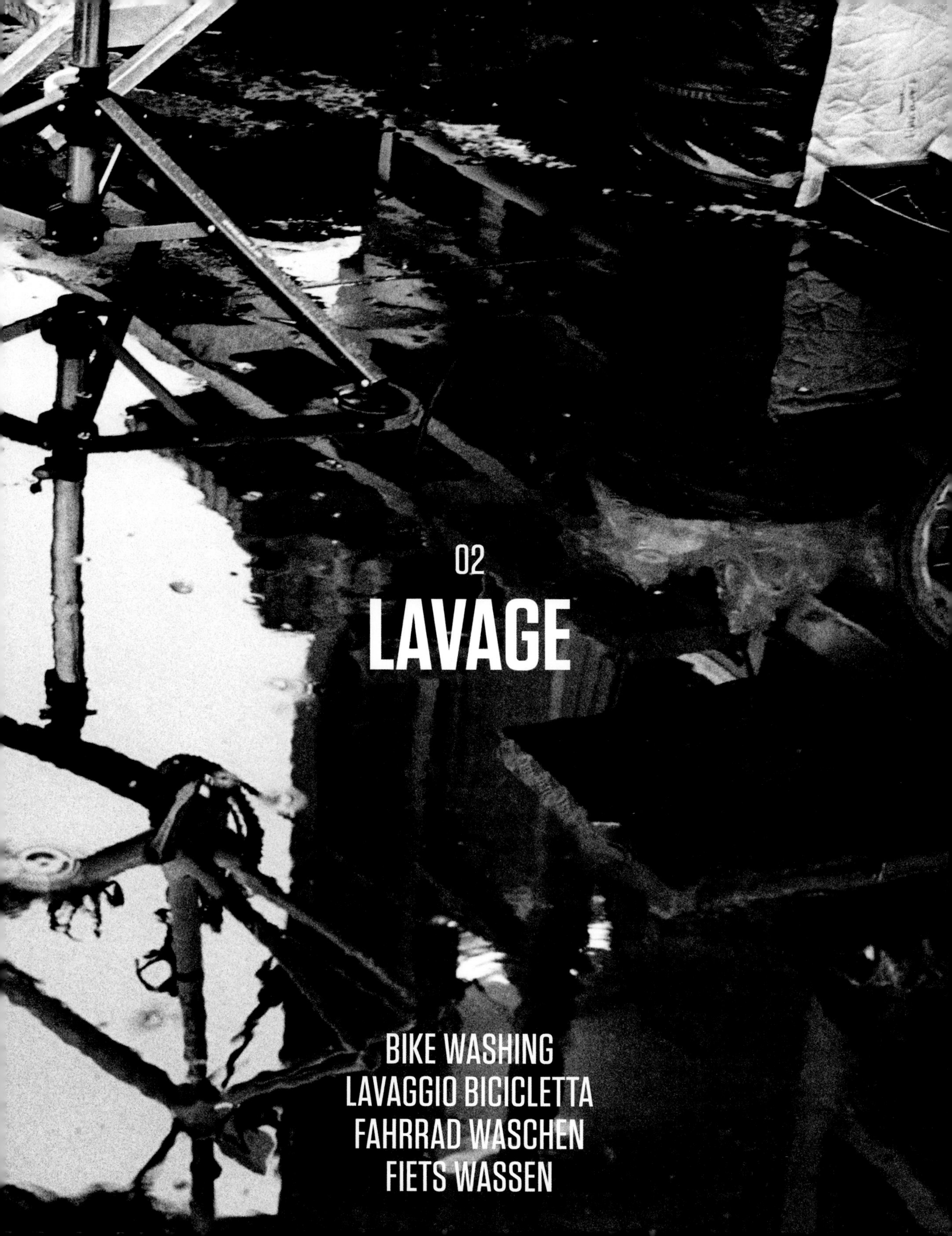

02
LAVAGE

BIKE WASHING
LAVAGGIO BICICLETTA
FAHRRAD WASCHEN
FIETS WASSEN

The routine of race day always ends up with bike washing

The first thing the team chef might do on arriving at the hotel is find the kitchen and check out the pans, but the first thing a mechanic does is find a water tap and park their 20-tonner right next to it. Water supply is essential. Compressors are fired up, jet washers unloaded and the trucks open up.

Alberto Masi was barely 16 when he escaped Milan and ran away to the bike races. He had special permission to work for a team at the Giro d'Italia. It was 1958 and tyres were still pumped up by hand, albeit with a track pump. Silk tyres and delicate treads needed very careful attention and partial deflation every day to retain their shape. So Alberto's first task as a professional mechanic was to inflate around 100 tyres each morning. It was exhausting but he didn't care—he was rubbing shoulders with his heroes, men like Ercole Baldini, Louison Bobet and Fausto Coppi and, better still, he was fixing their tyres.

The life of a bike race mechanic inevitably means a fair amount of routine work, although these days the tyres are inflated by compressors and they don't need as much care and repair as they did in the 1950s. That said, there is one thing that has always been and remains a part of their daily toil — bike washing.

Aside from team tidiness, repetitive washing has the main benefit of keeping wear and tear to a minimum. With no chance for gunk to build up on the drivetrain or rainy brake goo to trouble the frame tubes, cleaning is quick and easy. Washing a bike that has already been recently cleaned is a lot easier than trying to clean up your winter training bike (see page 261 for details of how to wash your bike in the home workshop.)

At the finish of a race all the team mechanics will need to get involved in washing the bikes. Most dress in fishing waders or, at the very least, wellington boots. It's a hectic time, and spillages can happen. It's all about getting the job done as quickly as possible.

The wheels are removed first, and washed separately — far away from the powerful degreaser that can soften the tubular glue and even rot away the cotton sidewalls. Cassettes are washed usually over a bucket with a bio degreaser.

The first washing mechanic then usually moves to the drivetrain, degreasing it with a powerful degreaser. Using a small stiff brush stored in an old drink bottle, degreaser will be slapped onto the moving parts.

The bike is then passed to another mechanic who may work the machine over from top to bottom with a bigger brush and some car washing soap. After that the suds and all the degreasing gloop are removed with a power washer. Unless the race has been particularly wet or muddy, the power washer is usually set to a fairly low setting. At a cyclocross race usually the only requirement is a power washer — the first degreasing step is hardly necessary when the bike is covered with mud.

Once the bike is clean another mechanic grabs hold of it as quickly as possible and transfers it in to a stand to dry it off and chase away all the water, usually with an air line. All the pivots in the brakes, the gears and even the rollers in the chain are blasted to make sure no water can begin to rust away at any steel parts.

The last mechanic in the line will thoroughly check the bike — especially the brake pads and cables — and will have to replace the rear wheel and run through the gears.

After the team bikes are done, any spare bikes may well need to go through this process, especially if the weather has been bad and they have been on a team car's roof rack all day. Finally the team cars themselves, buses and trucks all get a wash, all ready for the start of the next stage.

At one day races the washing may well be done at the finish, so they can pack up straight after. On stage races they usually take the bikes back to the team hotel to wash them there.

Team mechanics will split the workload. One washes wheels, one frames and gears, one rinses and dries. Then a lube and check over. It may look chaotic but it's a well practised routine.

Jet washers have certainly sped up the process, but they are noisy, wasteful and eventually break down. Pro teams use them for speed, but amateurs shouldn't.

A full roster of team bikes will take a good two to three hours to wash and prep properly. Then there's all the mechanical issues to iron out…

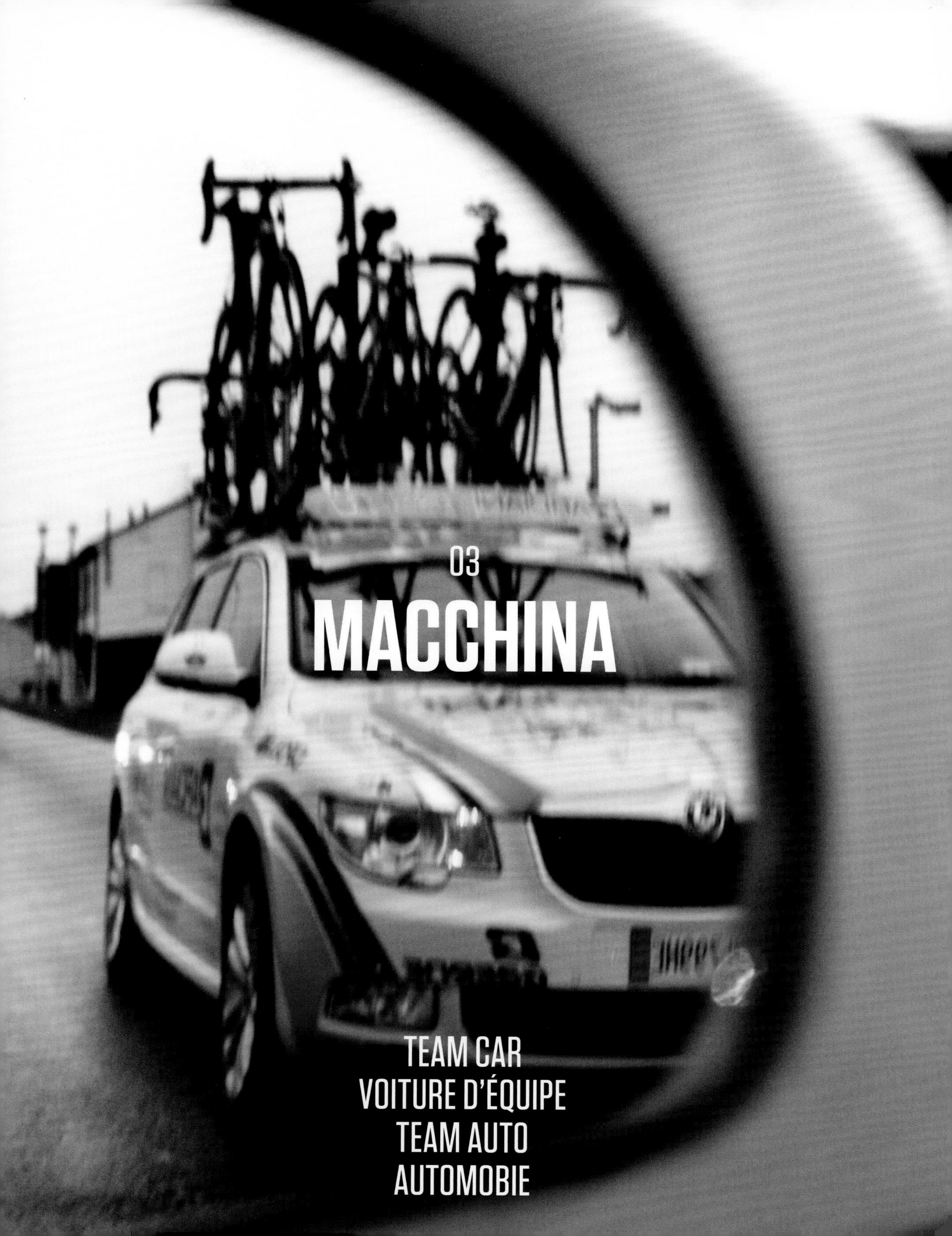

03
MACCHINA

TEAM CAR
VOITURE D'ÉQUIPE
TEAM AUTO
AUTOMOBIE

The mechanic always sits on the back seat, the right side

Mechanics get very little time to fully relax. Roger Theel (left) is Fabian Cancellara's main mechanic. The biggest and busiest day of his year is Paris-Roubaix: it is the race with the most problems, the most punctures, the most crashes and the most stress. Yet ask any mechanic to name their favourite race to work on and Paris-Roubaix will be it.

The race cavalcade consists of the team cars, press, sponsors, VIPs, race organisation, *commissaires*, directors, police and the neutral support. In the Tour de France, you're looking at a traffic jam of hundreds of cars. The media contingent alone is around 2,500 journalists, some 250 photographers and more than 50 TV crews. Add in the publicity caravan of around 200 vehicles and logistics crews, technical support, team coaches and trucks, and the carbon footprint of your average ProTour bike race would probably raise more than an eyebrow or two at a climate change conference.

The queue of cars at the start line is a formidable sight. The vehicles are crammed with technology — radios, fridges, televisions and special sunroofs over the rear seats through which passengers can shout. The Mavic cars take second place in the line, just behind the red car of race director Christian Prudhomme. The director and race *commissaires* have hotlines to all the team cars and the Mavic cars, enabling them to call team vehicles forward to assist a rider. Usually a rider raises a hand or drops back to the *commissaire's* car to ask for permission to take assistance from the team vehicle: whether that assistance is taking on *bidons* and food, or dropping off a rain jacket.

Stopping the team car or accelerating through the bunch requires experience, skill and judgment in equal measure. It also needs to be a singularly decisive process: barking orders to another driver would never work. This may be the main reason team *directeurs* take the wheel themselves.

Most race convoy drivers are ex-racers and, when you experience the driving up close, it's easy to see why. Immediate reaction time is necessary to be in control of the situation and react exactly at the moment you are called.

I have sat alongside such drivers when providing mechanical support on cycle races held on circuits and been suitably terrified, but the skills needed in the travelling support rally that follows a Grand Tour are something rather special. I say "rally" with qualified reason: the average driver in the peloton has to be navigator, timing expert and driver rolled into one. Meals have to be taken at the wheel, conversations completed with one eye on the road. It's a mass of multi-tasking, all carried out at exhausting speed. The neutral support team does all this, and they have to be mechanics too. When you experience the driving up close, it's easy to see why.

The rules of the road are left at the start line and the police wave you on to speeds unheard of in built up areas. It's pretty remarkable that there aren't more accidents. Sometimes it's a miracle that everyone gets home in one piece — near misses are inevitable.

It's incredible how the supporting cars manage to get to the finish in one piece too. These vehicles take pretty much the worst abuse you can give a car: plodding up hills, clutches frying, and then screaming down them. And, like the riders, they have to go through it day after day.

Neutral race support from Mavic and Vittoria

The idea of a neutral support car seems a little odd in the cutthroat world of bike racing. Nowadays assistance from team cars plays as much a part in the team's tactics out on the road as having a leadout train in the closing kilometres does, so to have 'outside' help may appear like they've got it easy. When Henri Desgrange started the Tour de France the whole idea was that the riders would be self-sufficient out on the road. Cycling has changed a lot in the last 100 or so years.

It was in 1889 that two French engineers from Lyon, Charles Idoux and Lucien Chanel, founded a firm called Mavic (an acronym for Manufacture d'Articles Vélocipédiques Idoux et Chanel — rough translation: Idoux and Chanel making bits for bicycles). Henry Gormand bought the company in 1920 and set about diversifying into wheels, and it produced the world's first aluminium rim. In time it became the rim of choice in the peloton. After Henry came his son Bruno, a man with massive ambition and enthusiasm for the sport.

Gormand Jr. was responsible for many new products but arguably his most inspired moment came when he turned the idea of race support into a marketing plan.

It came about partly by chance. A team *directeur* at the 1972 Critérium du Dauphiné Libéré found himself with a broken down car before one of the stages. Bruno Gormand lent his own car to the unfortunate fellow, and thus the idea of having a Mavic-branded car in the race convoy was born.

Races had long had a support car of some description — even amateur races have always had a volunteer driving a car full of spare wheels — but the idea of a fully professional neutral service car at the biggest races was an innovation. The idea was that Mavic would supply any rider with spare wheels and bottles while on the move, allowing team cars to remain behind the peloton. Gormand's original plan of acting as *directeur* to every rider was good for racing: it unclogged the dangerous roads around the peloton and ensured that only a few cars needed to be at the head of the field.

That's why Mavic is today probably most famous for its yellow cars. But why on earth would you choose yellow as a corporate colour? The simple truth is that Gormand was advised it would look better on TV than red, the colour of Mavic's previous logo.

Our man from Mavic is Frédéric Bassy. Frédéric was once a first category French racer — "Not bad, but not good enough," he tells me. So he switched from racing to the driver's seat of the neutral support cars and the mechanics' workshop. Being a former rider, he knows something of how the peloton moves, so navigating through the really, really tiny gaps is second nature to him. The drivers have to have an element of trust from the riders too — instead of quick changes in direction or sudden braking, you have to slip through the riders, like moving through a flock of birds or a shoal of fish. But there also has to be some authority and a pushy mentality from the driver too, so the horn is in constant use, as a combination of warning and, sometimes, excitable Gallic impatience.

Frédéric previously drove press cars and became great friends with the General Director of the Tour de France Christian Prud-homme. "I was Prudhomme's driver when he was a journalist with L'Équipe," he says. "I've driven cars for teams, race directors, VIPs and now for Mavic." He was also a mechanic for CSC when his compatriot Laurent Jalabert was on the team.

Neutral support cars need to be loaded with spare bikes and wheels each morning. The job can be stressful, dangerous and thankless. It requires a cool head and quick brains, so Vittoria's staff are a mix of ex-riders and shop mechanics. And a tax advisor…

**UCI CYCLING REGS
PART 2—ROAD RACES
ART. 2.6.033
TEAM VEHICLES**

"Only one vehicle per team will be permitted to circulate at race level. However, in races of the UCI WorldTour and of the continental circuits of the classes 2.HC, and 2.1, a second car per team is allowed, except in circuit races and on final circuits."

Frédéric tells me that there are no volunteers here and all Mavic personnel are paid. "There's only one race I'd do for free and that's Paris-Roubaix. But the reasons we are paid is to do with insurance and working with professionals on the continent—we need to be professional too."

If a cyclist signals for mechanical attention, race radio will call out his details using the native tongue of the rider's team (English for Sky, Flemish for Topsport Vlaanderen, French for Europcar and so on). Even so, at the Tour it is generally French which dominates the airwaves and there is no better race radio than that provided by ASO, the Tour organisers. In one day races, the big issue for the teams is not being close to the action at the front of the

race. In the Tour, there is no such problem: as soon as the break has gained 30 seconds the car will be there whenever they need it.

As long as, that is, they don't appear to be receiving too much attention. This is where neutral support steps in. They have at least two cars and two motorbikes at all races, so it is possible to have one car with the peloton and one behind, with the motorbike on hand should a second escape develop. Coordinating all this and ensuring all angles are covered requires a fair bit of concentration.

The job of neutral support is to be there always. Theirs is a job of impartial assistance but it is no surprise to discover that the Mavic crew, led by our driver for the day Frédéric Bassy, are a well-connected bunch (a short

Neutral race service is all about being prepared. Experience is essential — this is no place for a shop mechanic. Race logistics are pretty complicated for teams and neutral support. Tyres, bikes and wheels are constantly moved and rearranged.

walk through the team cars at the start is evidence of their popularity) and they are known by all of the directors and their coaching staff. That means that while team cars may come up to the breakaway to collect or hand out stuff, or simply to review the situation, they will invariably drift back to the peloton unless their team leader is involved — in which case Mavic is nursemaid to the team's riders remaining in the peloton.

The radio crackles into life and we are called forward to the break. Water is required. Because the Mavic car can't be stocked with every team's *bidon*, the usual routine is that the racer will hand his empty *bidon* to the support car, they will fill it with water, and it will be passed back strong-arm, 'sticky bottle'-style

so that the rider can sling himself back into the action. This time there is a slight misunderstanding (or perhaps we are just going too fast) and the system is ignored: the rider grabs the bottle of water, shoves it into his pocket, and returns to the break to refill his *bidon*.

After spending an hour or so break watching, the second Mavic car takes over and we have a chance to tuck in back behind the peloton. But there's a problem. The peloton has split in two following a crash, provoking mayhem, and there's a counterattack to contend with too. Once again, there's the call forward, and Frédéric looks a little worried for the first time. The race director wants him to move in between the split — that means overtaking the back half of the peloton and slotting

into the gap. We may then be called further forward to attend the countermove.

There's a different sense of speed now. We have riders all around the car — like monkeys at a safari park, they seem to be hellbent on swamping us — and they are noticeably twitchy, peering ahead to see where the split is. They don't look as relaxed and in control as the breakaway did a few hours earlier. There is a real feeling of urgency and, as Frédéric forces his way to the front, it is clear that there is little room for concession. Not for the first time, I'm squeezing my door handle a little tighter.

Totally out of the blue, Frédéric shouts: "Campagnolo, rear, 11 speed!" I have no idea how he spotted it — the break is flying along,

heads down — but Moreau is now noticeably slowing with a softening rear tyre and pulling off to the right of the road. The mechanic in the back grabs wheels from the seat beside him and Frédéric aims the car at the verge and onto the grass out of harm's way. The break has just over two minutes, so the chances of the Frenchman getting back in are slim. The doors are open before the car has stopped. Frédéric hops out and the wheel is removed. Moreau is calm, familiar with such inconveniences. By the time the change is done and Moreau is pushed away, the first part of the bunch has caught us and, soon after, the back group too. We, like Moreau, are back to square one.

In no man's land, support is needed yet again. The race is splintering and even the

Like many of the Vittoria personnel, Francesco Villa (below) raced as a youth. He started out as a mechanic for Claudio Corti's Gatorade team in the Gianni Bugno era. After leaving Gatorade, Francesco worked for many other pro teams, including Polti, Mapei, Quickstep and finally BMC in 2011.

Mechanics like Francesco have an idea of the hardship that riders need to endure. If it's cold they even help them get dressed.

Offering advice and reassurance isn't in the job specification but riders appreciate the experienced and knowledgeable support.

"I was just hoping for it to end, and that no-one got hurt. I'm an experienced motorbike driver for 13 years now at many important cycling races, but I never saw anything like that. It was exhausting, both physically and mentally."

ALBERTO GALBIATI, VITTORIA NEUTRAL SERVICE MOTORBIKE RIDER, ON THE 2013 MILAN-SAN REMO

back markers must be catered for. The parity in the support is commendable and sporting. We have no chance of getting back into the fray, so Frédéric decides to take a detour. Within a minute he's worked out the route — and that we have less than 10 minutes to cut the circuit and rejoin in the right position. Just a quick chat with a policeman to open the road and we're flying down a farm track at 140km/h. Frédéric pulls his seatbelt over his head (it's been fastened behind him to stop the alarm sounding). Through a village and down a hill, the car drifts from side to side — I'm just hoping this isn't for my benefit.

I may have been scared but professional riders show no fear of the cars which move alongside them. It's like being in a packed football crowd, the way that everybody moves as one, close but rarely touching. Frédéric points at the speedo while chatting into the radio and eating a sandwich: we're doing 80km/h and the riders are still spinning out a tempo, pedalling fast towards a hard left turn. He takes the corner with his knee, sandwich in mouth, so he can change down. From nowhere, a cyclist appears in the window at my right shoulder and, as Frédéric brakes, he uses our wing mirror to catapult his momentum forward, like a Six Day sling. I'm not sure if I'm impressed, terrified or both. No-one else in the car seemed bothered. All in a day's work.

The rules surrounding team cars and support vehicles are suitably complicated. For

"It was so cold I started losing sensitivity in my hands. At a point, I was forced to tell the *commissaire* that I would not be able to intervene if they had called for me because my hands were useless."

PAOLO TOMASELLI, VITTORIA NEUTRAL SERVICE MECHANIC, ON THE 2013 MILAN-SAN REMO

a classic or one day race, just a single car is permitted per team. For a Grand Tour, teams will have two cars following the race — unless it's a really narrow road, a mountainous stage, circuit finish or a time trial. While squads may bring five or more cars, minibuses and vans to any race, most of them are the worker ants, ferrying equipment, food, *soigneurs*, sponsors and mechanics to feed zones or vantage points along the race route.

The first team car in the convoy is always that of the World Tour leader. The order of the cars behind is generally decided by a lottery. Fail to provide a list of your riders' names beforehand, however, and the rules mean you are guaranteed a place right at the back of the string.

The day before the race, the *directeurs* and organisers have a meeting. Discussions are as much about who gets a lift with whom and where they can and can't be dropped off as they are about the race itself. It comes across like an over-complicated school run.

There is only so much space and so many pairs of hands that can assist riders. On a Grand Tour, two cars per team means around 50 to 60 vehicles following the peloton. When a break gains that magic minute's advantage, the team's lead car — complete with shouty *directeur sportif* — can come past the peloton to assist their rider. Or, as the more cynical among us would argue, grab some good publicity.

While each team is only allowed one team car behind the peloton at a single day race

such as this, out on the course there may be a few more, At Paris-Roubaix or the Tour of Flanders, for example, you can see dozens more team cars, minivans and motorbikes with spare wheels and bottles—but they are not allowed to officially follow the race.

At the Tour de France, the doubled team car allowance means each team can have a car behind the breakaway and one behind the peloton. In a race situation, this is where matters can get confusing and chaotic. If the remaining car drops back to help a rider, for instance, that leaves the rest of the team's riders exposed. If there's a crash, it can hold up that valuable second car too, leaving the team exposed and subsequently stuck way back in the race convoy.

A crash will block the whole road, creating congestion and frustration for the team cars. Riders are trained to go to the right hand side of the road if they puncture or experience a mechanical problem but this rule quickly gets forgotten in the event of a crash. Team cars and neutral service cars will always stop on the right, however. And while riders speak to their *directeur's* left hand side of the car, on the road fixes by the mechanic are performed out of the right window. It all becomes somewhat of a mobile ballet on wheels and is, perhaps, the most dangerous time for riders and team personnel.

It is strictly forbidden for riders to hang on to the team and neutral support cars: it is an action punishable by a fine. Of course,

Paris-Roubaix is undoubtedly Mavic's finest hour. The Mavic motos are in radio contact with one another and the drivers have notes on the equipment each team is using taped to their backs (see previous spread) This helps the pillion mechanic know which spare wheel they may need should they puncture.

it can be completely necessary when a part of the bike is being adjusted or when receiving medical attention and so in these instances a blind eye is turned.

Teams and riders will stretch the rules in other ways. The most common is what is known in the trade as "a sticky bottle" — a rider holding on to the bottle or energy bar being handed to them a little longer than they need to, meaning they get a sling back in to the race. A recent trend is for a mechanic to fix a flat tyre and then catch up with the stricken rider to feign some type of adjustment to the brake tension screws or perhaps to straighten the rear brake. The valuable few seconds' tow that the rider gets may just help them reattach to the peloton with slightly less effort.

I'd previously thought that neutral support did the bare minimum and were mainly there to look like they helped: sponsorship, endorsement and advertising being the overriding reasons for attending. But then I spent a day with the Vittoria neutral support at the 2013 Milan-San Remo. It was a very hard day, one which needed clear heads and quick hands and on which the neutral support went above and beyond.

While Mavic's yellow livery has become synonymous with the Tour de France, and Shimano's blue cars are becoming increasingly common in races across Europe, Vittoria has made the Italian races their own. The white Škodas of this Italian tyre manufacturer are always on hand at events like the Tour of

The climb of Plan de Corones on the individual time trial stage 16 of the 2010 Giro d'Italia was so steep — around 24 per cent at its steepest — that the team car's clutches couldn't cope. So team mechanics had to find a motorbike and a driver to follow their charges. Some of them even carried spare bikes.

Neutral support's driving skills have to be excellent. They spend a considerable time in the race itself, so concentration and multi-tasking at the wheel is a prerequisite.

Nature calls… Team cars and neutral support all have to stop at some point on a long classic race or stage. Finding a spot without spectators can be problematic.

It's not just races like Paris-Roubaix where navigating the roads becomes problematic. During the 2010 Critérium du Dauphiné stage to Sallanches in southern France, Mavic neutral support had to switch to motorbikes to stay in touch with the peloton during the tight and narrow finishing circuit.

Lombardy and the Strada Bianche, and are now a familiar sight at the Giro as well.

Servizio corse is usually the term for the storage unit or team headquarters for road cycling teams, but can also, somewhat confusingly, refer to neutral race support cars too. Vittoria's *servizio corse* manager Dario Acquaroli is an ex-professional mountain biker and knows he's lucky to have been spared a tricky induction into civvy street.

"I know a lot of ex-professional riders. If you save money when you are riding you can buy a little bar, or maybe a bicycle shop, but very few can work for a team. It's a good to know what riders do after their careers, because some have a terrible time. I am lucky because I have a job, and a job that I really

enjoy. Vittoria is an international company with different cultures involved. There is pressure and it's not always easy, but I like to work at the races.

"Diego Rosa [from the Androni Giocattoli team] wrote and thanked me for the help at San Remo. I was very pleased—we often do our work without receiving a nod; sometimes the team cars even yell back at us because they want to approach their riders while the Vittoria cars are sent by the *commissaires* to their place. Sometimes, a simple thank you can make your day."

04

LE CAMION

THE TRUCK
IL CAMION
DIE TRUCK
DE VRACHTWAGEN

The portable workshop

All pro team mechanics now use 'race stands' that have good solid bases and decent height adjustment. These allow the bikes to be washed and the gears to be run through very quickly. For heavy work there is usually a bench inside the truck, and sometimes a bench mounted workstand for more in-depth work such as removing bottom brackets or seized seatposts.

Race stands allow the bike to be spun around easily and can accommodate a variety of unusual frame designs and sizes. Best of all they pack away easily and can be stored in a small space or behind the seat of a car.

Team hotels on the ProTour circuit are perhaps the most varied collection of establishments in sport: from self check-in dives with pizza takeaways to ancient rambling chateaux with Michelin stars. No matter, as most of the time on the Grand Tours all the riders really want is a bed and a hot shower that works.

Out in the hotel car park, there's a slightly different type of requirement: space. At the smaller hotels, team buses and trucks squeeze into corral formation. In larger spaces, they stack up like holiday coaches, taping sections off to mark out their territory — space for the racks of team bikes and the work stands of the mechanics.

Workshop-based mechanics such as frame and wheel builders are often messy workers, leaving their workplaces resembling a teenager's bedroom. You will rarely see a messy team truck, however. Tidying is part of the job of a team mechanic — the constant breakdowns and build-ups of their workplaces mean they need to be organised and disciplined.

Along with kitchen facilities, washing machines and riders' kit bags stored in lockers under the floors, the team truck is home to a fully loaded repair shop, endless wheels and road and time trial bikes for up to nine riders per team. It's an impressive setup. If you were planning your dream bike shed, a ProTour team truck would fit the bill quite nicely.

Mechanics spend much of their time driving. When a team is at a Grand Tour, two mechanics will be in the team cars and another two will take the truck from hotel to hotel. Since there may be up to 10 teams staying in one hotel, they are very often on a race against time to get the best spot in the hotel car park. And then to organise an electric and water hook-up.

Typically the only time the truck will go to the start of the race is if there is a time trial. That way everything — wheels, bikes and turbo trainers — is easily available for the riders.

So being a team mechanic requires a little more than mechanical nous and a love of bicycles. You will also need a good knowledge of the bike races, an HGV licence and a strong sense for logistics.

Grand Tours go to some very beautiful places, but most days car parks and service stations are pretty much all a mechanic gets to see. The truck is a mechanic's home from home. They guard it well, so don't go asking to borrow an Allen key...

As much a part of the team as the bikes

Once upon a time race team mechanics were freelance. They had to use their own tools and drive their own car. This was stuffed with workstands, compressors, solvents, buckets and brushes. These hired hands followed the teams around from hotel to hotel and set themselves up. The process was hard work in itself and pretty inefficient, but that was the way until the teams started employing mechanics directly. These days team mechanics have a lot less to lug around to fix the bikes, but there seems to be a lot more material available too. Team trucks are better resourced and less has to be fixed on the bike, it may be all a bit more throw-away-culture, but safety of team riders is paramount, so replacing things is much preferred to keeping things going longer than their service life.

Some of the better resourced teams now have trucks with enough space for workstands inside, and we can expect these to become more popular. No doubt the mechanics will be delighted to be able to close the doors, turn up the stereo and put on the heating. There is no doubt that the jet washer

Truck facilities are certainly improving. Teams now have their own kitchen and sometimes complete restaurant on wheels. Team mechanics still spend most of their time outside, but the trucks are geared up for every eventuality.

It's important that you always want to make the best for the team — you have to finish the job, even if sometimes it is raining and it's midnight and you are still standing behind the truck and making the bikes ready for the stage or the race the day after.

RUNE KRISTENSEN

enabled team mechanics to speed everything up tenfold, and it seems that this will be the last thing that needs to be done outside, that is until they design an indoor bike wash. But there's a part of the bike racing scene that the fans like to see, and that's team mechanics fixing pro team bikes in the outdoors. If you can't get to see Tom Boonen and Mark Cavendish, seeing their bike being fixed up is the next best thing.

The costs of running two 18 ton trucks are pretty much the reserve of the top teams, for example Team Sky spend around €300,000 per annum on vehicle expenses and when a team coach can cost anything up to €1 million it's no surprise to hear that team below ProTour level still manages with a transit van.

Seeing the sunrise and set is pretty standard for a professional team bike mechanic. They often eat late and go to bed later. Being in the outdoors is OK, but working into and through the night is often on the cards, and when it's cold and wet a hotel with an underground garage is often a luxury.

05

SERVICE COURSE

TEAM GARAGE
SERVIZIO CORSE
SERVICE KURS
DIENST CURSUS

Much like your local bike shop, just with more stock

Whenever you're asked if you should buy a secondhand bike from a team at the end of the year, the reply is always: "Would you buy a second hand car from a taxi driver?"

Every professional cycling team needs a headquarters—a place where they store everything needed to keep 30 riders on the road. At the service course there's everything you can imagine you'd need, from spare team bus toilets to bed mattresses and bottles of water to physiotherapy supplies. There are shelves full of jam, washing powder and chamois cream. Toothpaste, beer and bleach. It's a bit like a bike shop mixed up with a supermarket, without any tills.

And that's not even mentioning the tools, the spares, and the bikes.

Riders usually have four team-issue bikes. They keep one at home and three—including a time trial machine—stay at the service course. Some riders will have more. Time trial specialists, for instance, will usually have two TT bikes. There are usually cyclo-cross bikes and mountain bikes kicking about too, for winter training and off-season racing. And of course the Grand Tour GC riders may have a yellow and a pink version of their racing bike, perhaps.

These days riders do not have to travel with their machines to races. The bus will bring their bikes prepped and ready to roll. Most teams will also bring along fresh kit, helmets, even shoes, so all the riders have to do is remember to bring their toothbrush. Spoilt, they are, spoilt.

Since the service course is where all the storage and bike building happens, most of the mechanics will live local to it. That's even the case if they hail from Australia and the service course is based in Oudenaarde in west Flanders. As Bob Farley, veteran Aussie team mechanic says: "You have to be near the material". 'Material' is mechanic for bikes and components, so during the racing season Bob moves to Belgium, heading back at the end of the season for well-earned rest and, hopefully, some sunshine.

With so much of the team personnel based near by, the service course becomes a social centre for those involved with the team. Riders drop in after training rides for coffee and a chat, it's got a warm friendly feeling to it, just like your local bike shop.

Since the service course is a relatively functional space, it is often housed in an out of town industrial estate. The precise locations are often closely guarded secrets and there is unlikely to be any branding on the outside of the building. With the amount and value of kit required to run a team, security is a big issue these days—ProTour teams have been followed back to the service course to be ripped off. So an out of town location is sensible, also because it tends to offer convenient motorway access for big trucks and the team bus.

There is a general location for service courses, however: Belgium. This is even the case for UK-based teams. Team Sky have a satellite service course in Belgium. There are several reasons. First off is that the Spring Classics mean the first half of the racing season is almost exclusively in or near Belgium. Then there's the fact that many of the bike manufacturers and component suppliers have their European headquarters in either Belgium or Holland. Finally, teams historically recruit Belgian mechanics, *soigneurs*, directors and team logistics crew. Cycling is Belgium, as the saying goes. So to see a team preparing for the new season, naturally we headed there.

Professional bike teams need kit and lots of it

Omega Pharma—Quick-Step's service course is near Wevelgem in west Flanders, Belgium. It is a lot more like a team head office than an old school service course. Alongside the workshops and storage areas are offices, meeting rooms and a small museum with a collection of team boss Patrick Lefevere's favourite ex-team bikes. It's home to Johan Museeuw's Eddy Merckx from his final Paris-Roubaix victory in 2002. The bike still has a piece of tape on the stem with the *pavé* sectors marked, and is caked in good old mud from the Nord Pas de Calais region, just a few kilometres away from the Belgian/French border.

Dominique Landuyt has been a professional bike mechanic with Belgian teams since 1991. When we visit the Omega Pharma—Quick-Step service course at the start of the 2013 season, he's been building up the Specialized Tarmac SL4 and Roubaix team bikes for nearly two weeks. The mechanics have to assemble from scratch: each bike is built from individual components from the frame up, they don't just grab a box from the manufacturer and spin a pair of pedals onto

them. Each bike is time consuming because every rider has special requirements, everything from the handlebars and stem to the position of the brake controls. The preference in thickness of handlebar tape and strength of pedal spring release is all noted. There is a huge spreadsheet with all the information on it, from crank lengths to saddle choice — no two riders are exactly the same. Tall or short riders pose a whole host of fit issues, and when the team is only using stock frames there can be a fair amount of head scratching involved in working out how to get the rider to fit the bike.

Dominique lives nearby and quite likes this time of year — he gets to do a 'proper job' and isn't out on the road for weeks on end.

"The best thing about this job is that you see lots of different countries, the worst is when your kids are sick and you can't be with them." He talks as he works and it's clear he has huge enthusiasm for the sport that he grew up with. "My father had a little pro cycling team, he was *directeur sportif* for many years and through the years there have been a lot of riders and characters, but I've survived them all. I've seen a lot of hard races too. The best is always Paris-Roubaix but it can also be the worst day to be a mechanic, like in 1994, the year Andrei Tchmil won Paris-Roubaix, the weather was like a horror movie and the mud was stuck to the bikes like cement."

To be a good mechanic you have to be a lot more than just a hard worker; you need to be

constantly ahead of the game and know what innovations are coming. And you need to be resourceful. Good teams use good mechanics and good mechanics will keep good components going for as long as they can. Chains and cassettes will be replaced in accordance to the recommended life expectancy. That means chains will generally be replaced after 2,000–3,000 racing kilometres, depending on the weather and the type of rider (some wear components out quicker than others). Most teams will build around 150 bikes at the start of each season. As Garmin mechanic Kris Withington told me in 2009, they have to be careful with how they use kit — they can't just hand it out. "The first year that we did the Tour, we changed the chains on both rest days.

Last year we used two chains, put a new chain on at the start and another halfway. But generally we use the material until it's finished." Even so, pro teams are supplied with a large amount of kit by their suppliers.

But before we go any further with team support we need some historical context. Back in 1973 things were slightly different. The service course was usually the back room of a bike shop. It was the year Shimano launched their first pro level Dura-Ace groupset, at a time when Campagnolo all but led pro team component supply. For many reasons this was a brave step for the Japanese firm.

Shozaburo Shimano and Tullio Campagnolo both rose from impoverished

"I liked him. He would always be at the races. We assembled all De Rosa bikes with Campagnolo parts of course, so I knew about their components inside out. One day I suggested to them to modify the front derailleur cage shape by one millimetre so the chain shifts properly and doesn't drop. The Campagnolo mechanic looked at my suggestion and gave me a thumbs up. Two weeks later, it was out as a production model. Amazing. I always gave them my feedback, because they will use it. In return, Campagnolo gave me everything I needed at the races."

YOSHIAKI NAGASAWA ON TULIO CAMPAGNOLO

backgrounds to oversee powerful bicycle companies, and both shared a love of engineering and bikes. They shook hands when they met; perhaps through all their hard work they had earned each other's respect. Yet their meeting took place when the two companies were on a collision course following Shimano's move into bicycle racing.

Campagnolo couldn't have been very worried at first. Why would it be? As a brand, it was race-proven — a massive technical advantage over Shimano — but more importantly it had massive clout. In the closed world of European racing, Tullio Campagnolo was a powerful man. The more romantic cycling fans criticise Shimano's lack of history and an absence of a racing legacy, pointing to the

paucity of team support and success in major road races until Andy Hampsten's 1988 Giro d'Italia win began to loosen the Italian stranglehold. But in 1973, whether it was aware of it or not, Shimano was facing a fiercely guarded monopoly. The only way they knew how to do it was to sponsor a squad — at huge cost, no doubt. And so along with the groupsets that went to Europe was a team of product engineers. Then, as now, Shimano were there to learn.

Their first team, the traditional and fairly conservative Belgian outfit Flandria, could not have been a fussier team to sponsor. Its leaders were Walter Godefroot, the experienced Belgian champion, and rising star Freddy Maertens, the young, brash and hugely

talented sprinter who could challenge Eddy Merckx in a sprint.

Being from the heartland of Belgian cycling, the team expected to win. Impressed by the surprisingly well-finished Dura-Ace groupset, Flandria's influential equipment managers signed Shimano to kit out their bikes, helping change the consensus view that the Japanese firm was destined for the utility market. Among the new developments, Shimano added a spring into the pivot bolt of the rear derailleur, allowing it to swing about its fixing point. This meant the derailleur could cope with larger variations in sprocket size, eventually leading to the servo-pantagraph system which became the derailleur norm.

Back in the 1970s, racing bikes used closer ratios, and the gears were smaller jumps. That meant the Campagnolo single pivot spring system coped far better with the demands of the racing bicycle and environmental conditions; there was, quite simply, less to go wrong. As former Flandria team mechanic Freddy Heydens remembered: "We did have some problems. Those first Dura-Ace components were difficult to install and adjust and the chains kept coming off. It seemed riders never stopped complaining about the group."

Shimano was quietly ambitious and keen to learn more about road racing, so instead of making a PR fanfare to announce its arrival in Europe, the firm choose to simply circulate a few groupsets and drop a small band of

"The relationship between the bike manufacturer and the sponsor is very important, it's like a family. You need this relationship for the best results. The sponsor puts in the money, we supply the bicycles, and the riders put in the heart. You need to work together."

ERNESTO COLNAGO ON TEAM SPONSORSHIP

mechanics and engineers in at the deep end. The feedback took time. Shimano insisted on written reports from their representatives after every month of racing. One of the correspondents sending information back to the Sakai HQ was mechanic Hiroshi Nakamura, and he was clearly realistic about the components' limitations. "My first impression of a European road race was one of complete mayhem," Nakamura remembers. "It was not uncommon for components, Campagnolo and Shimano, to break, and I remember the beating that our Crane derailleurs took at Paris-Roubaix..."

In the 1973 pro peloton, one team rode Shimano, three Simplex or Huret, and nine Campagnolo. By the time Shimano took part in its first Grand Tour, the odds had evened

up a little. As former marketing and PR man Harald Troost explains, Shimano were always determined. "They'll do anything, anything that can help them to get an understanding of racing conditions and racers' needs. It's really hard to imagine, but the engineers come to the races in Europe and ask questions, they watch and learn, then they go back to Japan and a year later they come up with something that blows you away."

Nothing changes much at Shimano. The guys who got the ball rolling in the '70s are still there, and many of the senior staff have been at the company for most of their working lives, employed as development engineers, then managers, then directors. Masahiko Jimbo was once on the circuit in Europe, testing

prototypes and developing ideas with the professional mechanics and riders, Today, after more than 30 years' service, he is director of marketing. Hiroshi Nakamura is now director of Shimano's bicycle museum. Such lifelong allegiance to a company is, of course, pretty standard practice in Japan. But this is also what makes Team Shimano a fascinating and highly effective machine. For example, a handful of guys controls its entire worldwide marketing. Several bike companies have 20 or more marketing executives, and here is Shimano, the biggest bike company in the world, with a marketing team that would fill a phone box. As Harald Troost explains, this is just how they do things. "The product always comes first. The idea is that when we make the product really outstanding, both in technical performance and in design, huge marketing efforts are no longer needed. The quality of the products is the best PR tool that we have."

Today Shimano are perhaps the biggest professional team supplier. Currently they support seven teams on the ProTour circuit, so going on standard bike supply levels that's about 1,000 groupsets, which is around €3 million's worth. Then there's wheels. Shimano also sponsor around 100 individual athletes for shoes and make bars and stems via their Pro range. Team sponsorship alone is a huge part of their global business and a large proportion of their marketing spend.

Campagnolo, meanwhile, remains the longest serving component name in cycle racing

"To develop bicycle componentry requires not only patience and skills, but experiences— not only good experiences, but bad ones too."

VALENTINO CAMPAGNOLO ON PRODUCT DEVELOPMENT

history. They built their name on supplying teams and have done every year since. Existing teams supplied by Campagnolo will already have a good deal of material and spares, but in a team's first year the supply is a bit larger to compensate for the lack of anything left over from previous years. At the end of each racing season, many riders will have to keep their old bike going until the new ones arrive in January. That means racking up thousands of kilometres in all weathers on it.

Having said that the team bikes will get brand new components for the first build every year and, with electronic shifting becoming the accepted choice now for most riders, all the big teams are looking for new groupsets. Campagnolo will supply 90 pairs

of their electronic EPS Ergopower shifters and 132 front and rear EPS derailleurs, then for stopping there are 90 pairs of brakes, and 140 sets of bottom bracket cups. 11–25 seems to be the most popular cassette choice, and the team will get 140 of them for a season, being the workhorse cassette ratio suitable for most terrain, however 11–27 and 11–29 are becoming more popular, as are the 52/36 compact drive cranks—essential it seems these days for riding up the Angrilu. Crank length varies from 170–180 with the most popular being 172.5mm and 175mm. Campagnolo supply 60 pairs of each crank length.

And they're not responsible just for kitting out the road bikes. Added to the list are 42 sets of time trial levers and EPS command

interfaces—essential for a team's TT bikes. Wheel-wise: 150 pairs of wheels with discs, with aero wheels and climber's specialist wheels making up a part of that. The teams will also use 29 pairs of standard hubs for handbuilding.

And what about tyres? I asked Kris Withington how many tubulars Garmin gets through in a season.

"We received around one thousand tubulars from Vittoria at the start of the year, including the special Pave tyres for the Classics. In the Tour, we get through around 60 to 70 standard racing tyres. It's enough to keep 50 or 60 pairs of wheels shod and ready for use. When they puncture, you always change the tubular. The guys will take that to the hotel and do it

while the race is still going on, so it can be ready for use the next day. We prepare all our spare tubulars at the service course in the days before a race. We use the tubulars until they're really worn—okay, so it'll go on the spare bike on the car, and one day it'll go on the spare wheel, and then it's pretty worn out, but there's always a few more days left in it.

"But this year, for example, David Millar, Ryder Hesjedal and Tyler Farrar—those three will every day have more or less new tyres. The *domestiques* will get the worn material, and they will use that material pretty much until they puncture. The best riders always get the new material, the best material, and the rest what's left. Because, at the end of the year, when we run three racing programmes,

"It was in 1972, we were exhibiting components at the Milan bike show, and at the time Shimano was nothing at all to European people, but our booth was next to the De Rosa booth. And every day I of course attend the show and I became friends with signor De Rosa—Ugo—and one day I asked him to make a bicycle for me. He checked my body size and everything, and several months later he sent me a complete bicycle—but [starts laughing] together with Campagnolo components! So you know I immediately changed to Dura-Ace…"

YOZO SHIMANO ON SHIMANO ENTERING THE WORLD OF PROFESSIONAL BIKE RACING

you'd run out of tubulars—especially if you're just pulling them off every day—so you have to be resourceful too."

Back at the service course, Omega Pharma—Quick-Step's Specialized bikes are equipped with SRAM's RED components. Although they may be relatively new to the road scene, they are fairly typical of a component supplier. So we asked SRAM what their average ProTour team gets through every year.

"Product is divided throughout team service course, several race trucks and the riders' home training material. There are usually 30 riders per team with around four to five bikes each, so all major teams run at least 150 bikes and we supply our current three ProTour teams in 2013 with SRAM RED groupsets (Omega Pharma—Quick-Step Pro Cycling, Saxo-Tinkoff Team and Cannondale Pro Cycling Team) and two of these (Saxo-Tinkoff and OPQS) we supply with Zipp Wheels and handlebar and stem products too."

Last, but by no means least, there are the spares. Over a season, a team will use nearly 300 chains and over 450 pairs of brake pads. They will get through several bearing sets and new tools specific to the latest developments, so each mechanic's tool and spares kit will be updated accordingly. Most teams will also get through a lot of bottles, around 25,000 in one year. Then there's the contact points: around 250 pairs of pedals and 400 saddles. Needless to say, then, running a team requires a lot of kit.

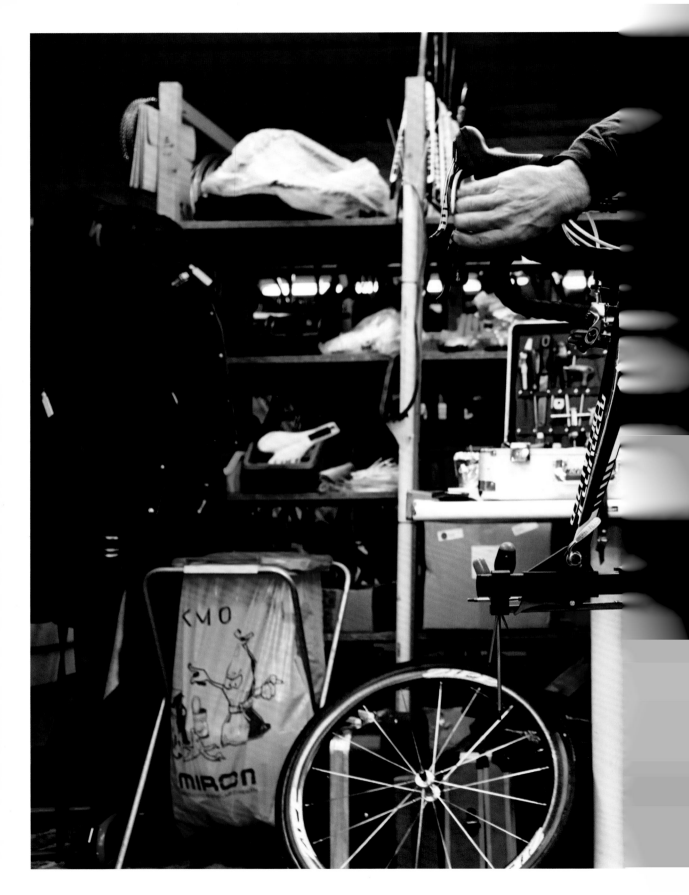

HARDWARE

06
TOOLS

OUTILS
STRUMENTI
WERKZEUGE
GEREEDSCHAP

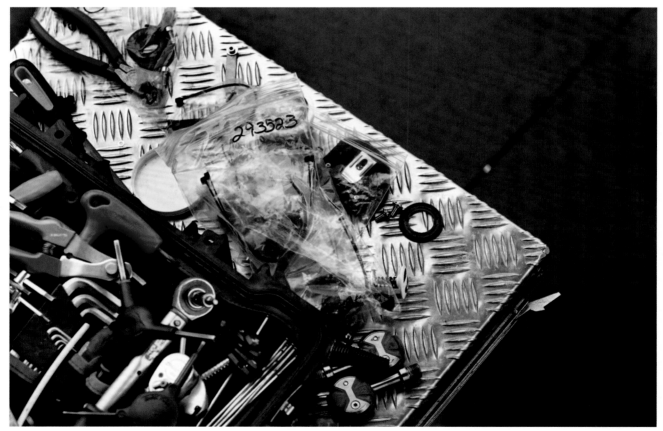

Cheap tools do cheap jobs

Not all tools are just bought off the shelf. Some have to be made or modified, like this podger.

Travel toolkits are essential for both professional and enthusiast mechanics.

All mechanics know that they should look after their tools…

In short, you simply cannot build a bike from scratch or service it properly without quality tools. They need to fit precisely and be durable so they wear out slowly and evenly over time.

Team mechanics usually have two or three sets of tools: one extensive kit that hangs on the workshop wall, one emergency box for taking in the team car, and often a slightly more comprehensive one that lives in the truck. Good mechanics pride themselves on the tools they have amassed. We hang on to apparatus for years — long after the component they were designed to install or adjust has been consigned to history — because you never know when it might come in handy.

Beyond the basic Allen keys, spanners and screwdrivers, it is vital to ensure you have access to specialist tools when preparing a frame for the first time. Bottom bracket bearings will only last if the frame is tapped out and faced properly; headsets will only fit into head tubes that have been readied for the cups or direct fit bearings to be installed. Carbon frames and forks need very careful preparation if they are to be assembled safely, so take care to use the correct cutting and preparation tools. Using a tool that isn't suited to the material is likely to result in frustration, destruction or both.

It is unwise to assume that a new frame will be problem-free during assembly. Checking frame alignment is highly recommended. All threaded elements on the frame should also be checked to make sure they are clear of paint or debris and also that they are in line. Likewise faces that are destined to meet components such as cups or bearings should be prepared correctly.

After use all tools should be carefully cleaned before putting them away. This is even more important where cutting tools are concerned. It means they will be ready for their next outing and also that any damage or wear and tear can be more easily monitored and acted upon. When storing fragile cutting tools it is good practice to hang them after use. If that's not possible, the next best option is wrapping them in a bit of clean rag, taking care to ensure that the delicate cutting edges do not come in to contact with each other or anything else that may damage them.

Tools should be looked after and used for their exact purpose: avoid the temptation to use the head of a pair of cutters as a makeshift hammer. If you visit a shop and see their set of bottom bracket cutters covered in grease, rattling around in a drawer or storage bin, you might want to get your threads chased elsewhere.

In reality your toolkit is never fully complete. As tools wear out with regular use eventually they will need to be replaced.

If you plan to carry out basic servicing on your own bike, invest in a workstand. Working at the correct height with the bicycle held securely will make a massive difference to the ease with which you can carry out certain tasks.

Campagnolo (and Royce) tools

Campagnolo tools are always the finest quality and design. A full Campagnolo toolkit in a wooden box is now a valuable collector's item with a price tag to match. Strangely many of the tools here will still be found in professional mechanics toolboxes, even though the bicycles using the components they service are long gone. Maybe it's simply nostalgia or security, but good tools are like old friends — always there when you need them.

(A) The Campagnolo UT-BB080 is the official tool for the installation and removal of Record and Chorus (and original Athena) square taper bottom brackets and all their 8, 9, 10 and 11 speed cassette lockrings. It needs to be used with a 24mm spanner or socket and is made from hardened steel which ensures a good fit and long life.

(B) The iconic Corsa Record (or C-Record) hubs had their cones concealed by beautifully polished alloy conical covers that streamlined their appearance and also helped to keep dirt and water out. These covers were held in place with small seven sided spring clips and are, in practice, difficult to remove without marking their mirror finish. This lovely hand tool from Campagnolo made removal much easier and is still a joy to use. It's much kinder than the edge of a cone spanner or the tip of a flat blade screwdriver.

(C) These three Campagnolo spanners are inseparable. Each assists the other in the installation and adjustment of traditional headsets and bottom bracket systems. From top-to-bottom: 32mm headset nut and adjustable bottom bracket cup, 15mm pedal axle and fixed bottom bracket cup, 32mm headset cup and bottom bracket lockring.

(D) High quality British component manufacturer Royce uses a peg and toothed spanner system to adjust their titanium square taper bottom bracket cups. The spanner is made to their own specific dimensions, necessitating yet another addition to the toolbox. It works well once held in place with a crank bolt and washer to prevent slippage.

(E) The Campagnolo Record Delta is arguably the most beautiful (and coveted) brake calliper ever produced. It needed extra care during installation, however, as well as constant monitoring of brake pad wear and a very patient mechanic. Perhaps the most frustrating thing about its design was the use of a 3.5mm Allen key for cable clamping duties: not the most common of sizes. I have a couple which are closely guarded and the red insulation tape makes them easy to spot in the toolbox or on the bench.

(F) Another specialist Campagnolo tool which looks just like a bit of bent wire — which essentially is exactly what it is. Indispensable when servicing older style 8 and 9 speed Campagnolo cassette hubs, this simple creation holds the pawls and springs in place during reassembly.

(G) You will need a specialist tool like the UT-BB100 when fitting Campagnolo's cheaper modular sealed bearing bottom brackets for square taper BB fitting chainsets. Thankfully it also uses a 24mm spanner for extra leverage.

(H) The 'Peanut Butter Spanner' still has a place in many mechanics' back pockets since its 15mm thin walled design fits most track bike wheel nuts as well as the 15mm bolt used on many square taper cranks. It allegedly earned its nickname as it was an ideal shape to scoop peanut butter — for years a popular and affordable source of energy for Six Day racers — out of the jar. Although there are many examples of this tool on the market today, Campagnolo's original design is still the nicest.

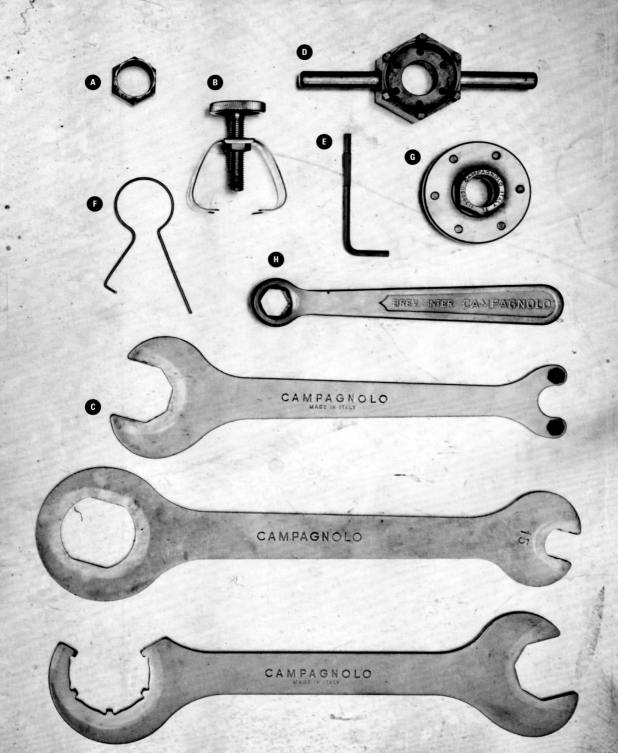

Allen keys and wrenches

The Allen key has been an engineering revelation and has transformed the toolbox of the professional bike mechanic. Spanners are heavy, hard to use and even harder to carry on a bike as an emergency repair option. So these days you can fix pretty much any bike with a few Allen keys and a chain tool. But be warned, multi-tools and cheap Allen keys aren't always the best solution as many bolts are hard to reach. A good set of Allen and Torx keys will help bolts last longer and, combined with a decent torque wrench, reduce assembly time.

A A quality set of Allen keys is essential in a professional's toolkit or workshop. These examples are made by USAG in Italy. Their precisely formed tips all but eliminate any chance of slippage or rounding off—they are a joy to use. Coloured tape will help identify sizes if you're always trying to find the right one. Some sets now come ready painted too.

B Ball-ended Allen key drivers are invaluable when you need access to awkward fittings such as bottle cage bolts. These handy tools also hasten the initial setup of many Allen head bolts on a bike.

C The UT-BB110 was added to Campagnolo's current tool range to assist in the correct tightening of their Ultra-Torque chainsets. The 10mm coupling bolt can be difficult to access with some commercially available torque wrench fittings, which are too short, so this extender overcomes the problem.

D This Campagnolo 5mm Allen key is one of my oldest tools and still used to this day. Its splined barrel makes it easy to rotate quickly and it has tightened and undone more chainring and seatpost bolts over the years than I care to remember.

E French-made VAR Allen keys are particularly high quality. Favourites of mine are their 8 and 10mm, with hardened shafts mounted in comfortable nylon handles that make stubborn pedals and crank bolts that bit easier to undo.

F Campagnolo's classic T-bar Allen key was an absolute must have for many years. This was the first ever specialist cycle-specific tool that I bought and it has sentimental value for that reason alone. Equipped with a 6mm handle and an 8mm socket, it's just small enough to gain access to the nuts on older brake lever mounting clips. The tips of this Allen key have been cut back and ground a couple of times so it still gets used to this day.

G Many manufacturers' fastenings on current components have seen the traditional Allen key abandoned in favour of Torx fittings. In the main this is due to fragile, lightweight alloys taking the place of steel. These light materials are much more prone to rounding out, but Torx drive all but eliminates this. These Beta drivers are comfortable, precisely formed and easy to spot in the tool chest thanks to their bright orange handles. T25 and T30 are the most regularly used on modern bikes.

H Everyone needs a multi-tool of some sort as it allows you to carry, albeit in miniature form, several tools in a portable package. This example from Wheels Manufacturing is another favourite and has the added bonus inclusion of an emergency gear hanger to help get you out of a sticky road or trailside situation.

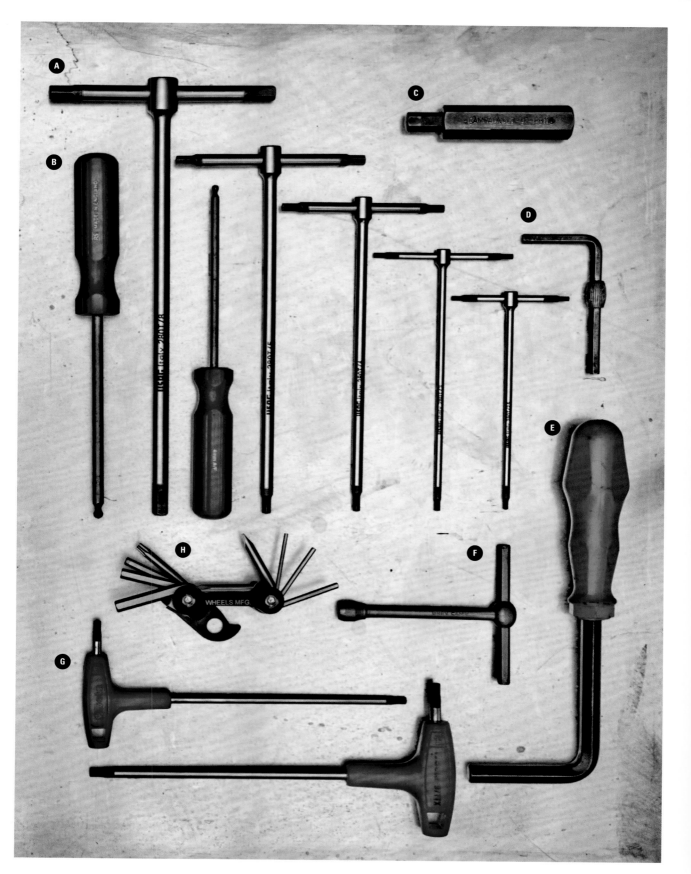

Pliers and pincers

Pro bike mechanics will only lend out their tools very begrudgingly. You might manage to borrow a track pump from a team truck, but mechanics will never lend out their favourite cable cutters — because they have to be carefully used and looked after.

When bicycle fittings had nuts and bolts that could be rounded off by uninitiated and ham-fisted mechanics, pliers had a pretty bad reputation. On the rare occasions you do need them these days, it's important that they are of the finest quality.

A Slip-joint pliers have myriad uses and can be pressed into service for obvious jobs when a standard pair of pliers won't do. I often find that front mech butchery — bending, squashing and squeezing into shape — is much easier with this tool, particularly when working on older bikes. As long as the jaws open nice and wide and have a reasonably compact head, any brand will do.

B A pair of generic 'mole grips' are a must have in any mechanic's toolkit. I sometimes wonder what life must have been like before someone invented this indispensable tool. Copied hundreds of times over, the design is pretty much the same as the original. Smaller jawed models can also be very useful.

C Park Tool cable cutters differ from conventional types thanks to their 'parrot beak'-style blades, and are a real boon when trimming modern gear cable housing. Instead of using a coiled lay-up, the gear outer casing features strands of wire that run lengthways to improve the consistency of gear change once adjusted. Normal cutters can shatter this PVC housing and spread the individual metal strands, rendering it useless. The tool shown cuts cleanly from all sides simultaneously, like a pair of shears.

D This pair of Facom 195.16G angled pin-nose pliers have a super-secure grip courtesy of their precision ground tips. I find myself using them on a regular basis, especially when faced with restricted access during jobs like extracting an awkward brake or gear cable inner wire from its lever housing.

E I try to have a mixture of tools from different brands with different handle designs which make for easy and quick recognition. I have a few hand tools from Beta and have found them to be good quality and quite distinctive. The ergonomic handles on these pin-nose pliers make them very comfortable to use and a favourite of mine for tensioning inner wires before clamping them in place.

F These Knipex cutters from Germany are absolutely fantastic and easily justify their hefty price tag. Based on the same basic design as a pair of heavy-duty bolt croppers, they make light work of brake and gear inner wires, brake outer casing, spokes and even — at a push and if approached with a bit of sympathy for the cutting edges — stainless steel mudguard stays.

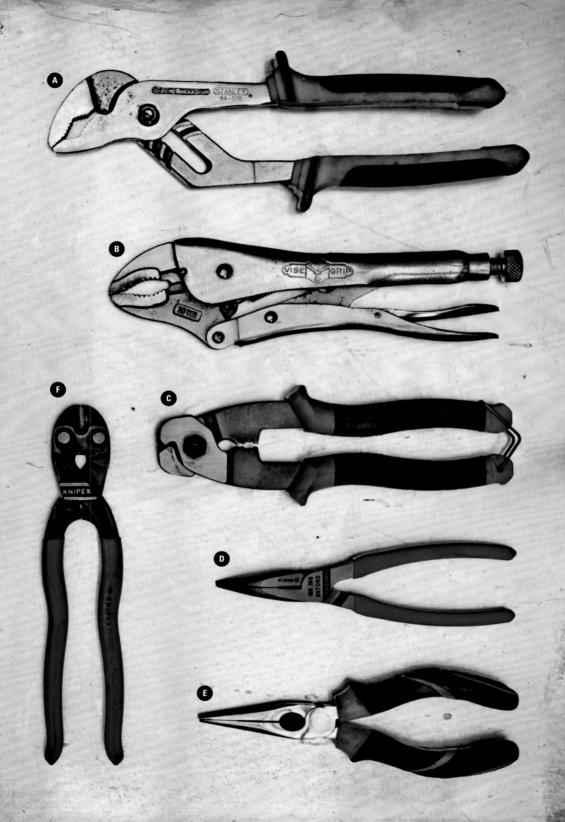

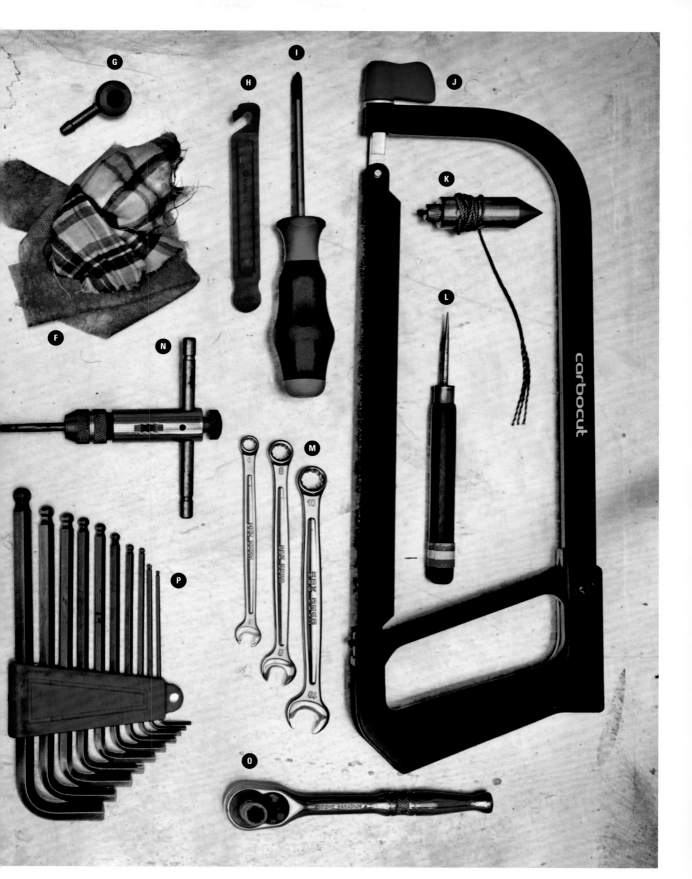

Essentials (previous page)

The extras that get regular use at a bike race are always hard to find in off-the-peg toolkits. Pro bike mechanics will customise their kits with favourite tools and things they pick up along the way. When you're miles from home, much of this stuff becomes essential for setting up a workshop in the basement of a hotel or in the car park of a race village. Like Boy Scouts, mechanics must always be prepared.

A It is important to avoid skin contact with the wide multitude of greases, cleaning solvents and lubricants that face today's professional bicycle mechanic on a daily basis. I use two different types of glove depending on the job in hand but these nitrile ones are my favourite, being 6mm thick for added durability and with a deep cuff to keep wrists and forearms protected too.

B Old brushes of any kind are invaluable. Save your old toothbrushes for intricate cleaning jobs and make sure you have some slightly larger, tougher brushes for heavier duty scrubbing activities.

C Insulation tape is another workshop essential, used for everything from anchoring brake and gear cables' outer casing in place to marking saddle heights before seat pin removal. Having a good supply with a few colour options for artistic handlebar taping detail is always helpful.

D Post-It notes are another workshop godsend. I regularly use them for noting down cutting instructions and rider measurement details. Saves you digging around for scrap paper or writing it on your hand then washing it off before realising you have just erased someone's fit data.

E A selection of grease gun attachments fitted to the tubes of your most popular lubricant means more accurate application and time, money and lubricant saved.

F You can never have too many cleaning wipes and rags. Old cotton T-shirts and Big Wipes (ready to use with solvent) are personal favourites.

G Disc wheel track pump adaptor. If you need to ask why, you don't need one!

H Tyre levers are of course another workshop indispensable. I have used dozens of different types over the last 30 plus years and feel confident when I say that the Campagnolo WH-009HYC composite lever is the best I have ever used. Lezyne and Park make reasonable alternatives.

I Screwdrivers are obviously another must have in any workshop or toolkit. You should always ensure that you have the right size tip for the job to avoid unnecessary mangling of the screw head. Two Philips-style and three slot head drivers will have most jobs covered.

J Cutting carbon fibre is a very specialist operation—a badly executed cut can have expensive and even dangerous consequences. The special blade on this CarboCut saw from Effetto Mariposa 'sands' through the fibres and produces a significantly cleaner cut than a traditional toothed blade, with no splintering. Make sure you wear a mask or use a method of safe dust extraction when cutting any carbon fibre component.

K A plumb-line, spirit level and tape measure are all you need to record and transfer bike fit data.

L This 'pointy thing', or podger, came from my granddad's toolbox. I straightened it years ago and now use it to clear and reshape the plastic liners after a cable outer casing has been cut. It's essential for smooth cable runs.

M A selection of high quality ring and open ended spanners is essential. I find a range from 6–17mm in 1mm increments covers it all. A ratchet-ended 8 and 10mm can also be very useful. Budget spanners often don't last long and they don't fit as snugly as quality spanners.

N Thread taps have several useful applications but their main purpose in most workshops is to clear paint or lacquer from threads on new or re-enamelled frames. Rear derailleur (10mm) ones for clearing debris from the rear hanger threads allow ease of assembly without forcing anything. Pedal/crank taps are also worth having.

O A ratchet set is a great workshop asset and is usually sourced with a multitude of sockets and bits to allow many awkward or repetitive tasks to be dealt with quickly and effectively. As with spanners, a quality set will last longer.

P Traditional Allen keys are still vital as there will always be occasions where bulkier versions with moulded handles are unable to get into awkward spaces. This ball-ended set from VAR is very useful and made from high quality steel.

Q 3 in 1 oil. It's not cutting-edge lubricant by modern standards but it has its uses. Every workshop should have a can.

R Acetone is invaluable when preparing carbon fibre rims for tyre gluing as it removes all traces of rim-mould release agent and leaves no residue. It is also useful for other chores and will often help remove unwanted graphics from certain items. It must be used with care, however.

S Amaretti Biscuits. It should be noted that these are not exclusive currency in bicycle workshops. You will be amazed how grateful a mechanic will be if you make a donation of any type of cake or biscuit. I have yet to see confectionary left uneaten in a workshop.

T Fibre grip, or assembly paste as it is often known, is an absolute must have for any mechanic in this age of lightweight and essentially fragile composite components. I use it almost everywhere that two surfaces are clamped together to reduce the amount of torque required and hold the items firm.

U Metal polish. Not as useful as it once was thanks to the proliferation of boring black components on modern racing machines but when you come across a dull alloy or chrome part that needs a bit of TLC, you will be ready.

V Chain lube is obviously something that every toolkit should have. Finish Line make some of the best lubes on the market, but as with any lubricant the secret is less is more. Remember, there is no point oiling something that is dirty—clean it first.

W Tape measure. You are always going to need one of these. Make sure it is good quality, legible and that the lock-out function is effective.

Fork and front end tools

A few components on a racing bicycle need specialist tools for installation and removal. Forks are the main area that will need these workshop tools. If you haven't got them, don't even try to bodge it. Fork breakages are usually the fault of installation or previous crash damage. Carbon forks are supremely strong and light but also very fragile and liable to damage from poor installation or incompatible tools. Always read the instructions and never cut corners.

(A) This fork headset crown race setter from Park Tool is a simple device. It essentially comprises a tubular driver designed to accommodate your chosen steerer diameter, combined with the relevant adaptor of your crown race (not shown as there are quite a few options). It is used as a slide hammer or persuaded with a hammer of some description to force the race squarely onto the crown of your forks.

(B) Cutting forks to size accurately requires care and skill but everyone at some time has experienced the wayward hacksaw blade. Park Tool fork cutting guides overcome this and make the process a breeze, providing several variants to cover all eventualities. The guide shown is intended for use with carbon fibre-specific saw blades and has a slightly wider opening between the guide plates. Simple and quick to use, it assists neat and accurate cuts.

(C) This VAR headset cup press has long levers, and a thrust race ball bearing makes light work of the installation process. Adaptors allow for fitting the various cup diameters.

(D) One of the most awkward jobs facing today's bicycle mechanic is the removal of old, damaged or worn fork crown races. In the old days most races extended well past the shoulders of the fork crown and so removal was often carried out with a hammer and punch. Modern designs are generally fitted against a crown that is larger than the race so there no easy way to prise it from its resting place. This fork crown race extractor from French toolmaker VAR is a life saver and turns a potentially difficult and time consuming task into a few seconds' work.

(E) Conventional headset cups, once pressed home, are very tightly fitted so removal is always something of a challenge. Sure you can improvise, but if you resort to using a punch it is very difficult to keep the cup square as you remove it. This expanding headset cup extractor from Park Tool is made from spring steel and, once snapped into place, will safely remove most cups with a couple of sharp blows with a hammer. A bit medieval but it works.

(F) Park Tool's star fangled nut setter is a simple but invaluable device that will install the nut into steel or aluminium steerer tubes with ease. Its rubberised outer cover helps to reduce jarring and provides a useful firm grip.

(G) Chris King makes the best quality headsets in the world, as well as some superb hubs and bottom brackets, so it is great he offers a range of dedicated tools for the installation and servicing of his products. It is imperative when pressing a King headset that no pressure is exerted on the bearings and that no tool mars the beautiful finish.

Chain tools and chain splitters

Professional bike teams get through a lot of chains. For every chain type it seems there is a chain tool and a recommended method of replacement that is sometimes so complicated as to border on the ridiculous.

As sprockets multiply, chains become narrower and subsequently more fragile and vulnerable from side loads. Chain breakages are rare and only result from using the wrong tools.

A The first generation Campagnolo 10 speed drivetrains had their own specific chain and individual method of installation. The Permalink was a flawed method of connection that, despite its name, was prone to much quicker wear than the other normal links in the chain. Not only did this installation require a special link, it also required a special tool. I bought one to comply with Campagnolo's strict policy on chain assembly but it quickly became redundant as the company launched a new and more reliable permanent pin system together with, you guessed it, another expensive specialist tool.

B The Shimano TL-CN33 deluxe chain tool is a thing of beauty and a pleasure to use. Its rosewood handles feel comfortable under load and are long enough to make light work of breaking or joining a chain. It features a neat steel chain holder that assists in the reliable insertion or removal of the relevant connecting pin.

C Park Tool was the first manufacturer to produce a device that assisted the removal of the new breed of easy release chain links. Its MLP-1 tool is good quality, comfortable to use and makes the removal of worn or slightly distorted master links a doddle.

D Campagnolo's UT-CN200 is another beautifully made tool, featuring a special clip to ensure the chain cannot move during the joining or breaking process.

E Chain manufacturing specialist Rohloff blazed a trial when it came to chain stretch checking devices. This example has been around for over 20 years. One side measures 0.075mm elongation, which alerts the user to partial wear of the chain. The 0.1mm elongation side shows when immediate replacement of the chain is needed. A simple, reliable tool that will save you money and minutes.

F This economical chain tool from BBB is a prime example of a useful, practical product being made easily available to the home mechanic. The BTL-55 allows the connection and removal of 8, 9, 10 and even 11 speed chains thanks to its ingenious adjustable width chain gate and link peening attachment.

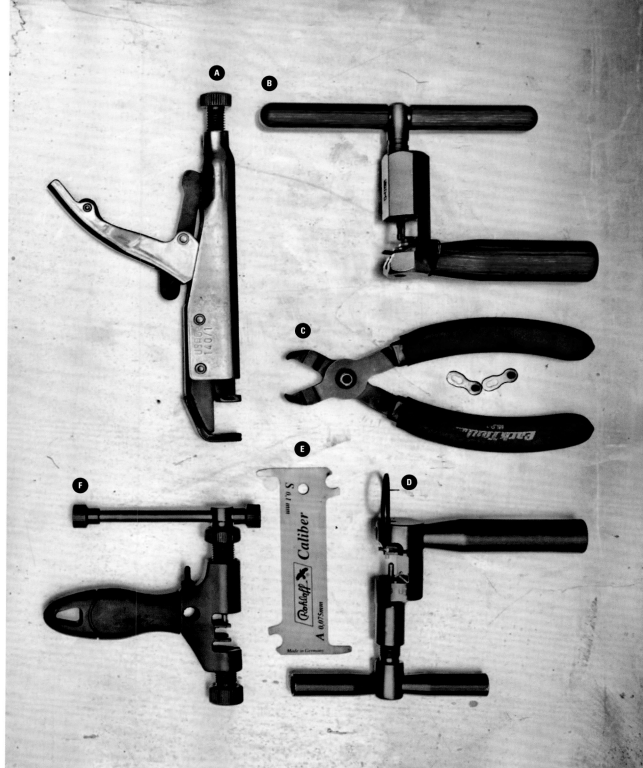

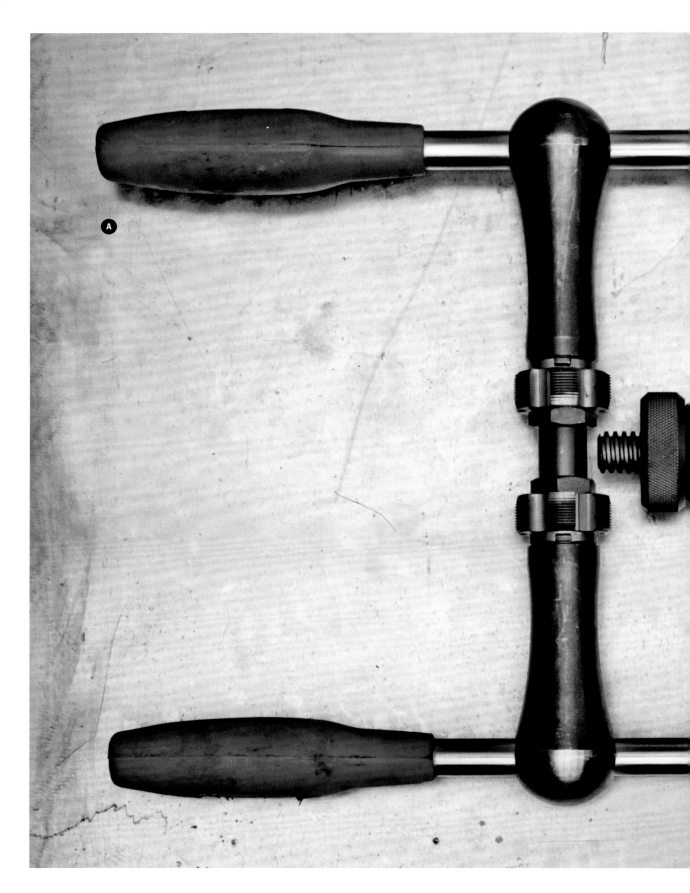

Bottom bracket tools (previous page)

Despite recent attempts by frame and crank manufacturers to convince us that pressing a bottom bracket bearing straight into the shell of a frame is best practice, many still firmly believe a traditional threaded cup is a better and more practical approach as it can be replaced if the bearing interface is compromised in any way. A far better option than having to trash a complete frame because the bearing seat is damaged.

A Threaded cups need careful installation. For maximum performance and bearing life, it's crucial to ensure the BB shell is clean and ready to receive the cups. This In line tap from Cyclus is available with BSA (1.370×24") or Italian (36×24) thread cutters and is used to clear any paint or debris that may prevent smooth and accurate installation of the BB cups. It also, as the name suggests, ensures that the left and right hand cups run in line, which is essential for the integrity of the bearing races.

B It is always worth checking a frame's bottom bracket shell faces, regardless of pedigree. Modern cups benefit from correct installation as much as their predecessors yet recent times have seen a slightly cavalier approach to this aspect of frame preparation. Both cups need to be tightened firmly in place to avoid creaking and to help get the best from whatever bearing system you choose. This BB facing tool from Park Tool uses threaded guides which are screwed in place (once the threads have been checked and corrected). The faces are then carefully skimmed, with only the bare minimum of material or paint being removed, to ensure that both surfaces are parallel and ready to receive the cups.

Headtube facing tools (next page)

If good frame preparation is overlooked bearings will wear out more quickly, and bearings are not something team mechanics will want to be changing during a stage race. Stripping frames and cranks takes time. Far better for them to need doing once in a while back at the service course rather than in a workstand outside the team hotel in the pouring rain. Bottom bracket bearings will easily last a season if fitted to a well-prepared frame.

A One should never underestimate the importance of correct headset fitting practices. Just like bottom bracket tools, the more care taken the better the bearings will perform and the longer the individual units will last. This Park Tool allows the user to prepare the head tube to receive the cups, which must be installed in the next phase of assembly using a dedicated press. The quick release conical lower section centralises the tool while the coil spring applies gradual pressure during operation. This corrects the internal surface of the head tube and ensures that the circular external face is perpendicular and parallel to its opposing surface.

B Modern internal headsets have, in some cases, done away with this practice. However, there are commercially available chamfered cutters that can and should be used to ensure that the conical bearing surfaces are clear of unwanted paint and surface irregularities.

Tightening and measuring

Many of today's high performance bicycle components are made from exotic materials and pared down to the absolute minimum in an attempt to reduce weight. For this very reason a cavalier attitude to manufacturers' assembly instructions is no longer an option. Every modern bike has fittings that have a recommended maximum torque setting and it is important to have tools that allow a wide range of different Nm ratings to be applied. No one tool will do — at least two will be needed. See page 266 for more on torque wrenches.

TORQUE WRENCHES

A Effetto Mariposa means butterfly effect in Italian. This Giustaforza ('correct force') torque wrench is beautifully made and its knurled body provides excellent feel. It comes with a multitude of bits and extenders, making it ideal as your main method of monitoring the tightness of your delicate carbon fittings. Rated from 2–16Nm, it has all but the biggest jobs covered.

B British firm Norbar is one of the industry leaders in the production of high quality torque wrenches. The large wrench covers the heavy stuff like bottom bracket cups, cranks, cassettes and the like while their smaller tools take care of fragile fittings such as carbon fibre seatposts, carbon handlebars and steerer tubes.

C This little gem from Ritchey assists you in setting any 4mm head fittings to 5Nm, making the fitting of your four bolt handlebar stem face plates a breeze. Use this in combination with assembly paste for safe installation of sensitive components like handlebars and seatposts. A version with removable 3mm, 4mm, 5mm and T20 bits is also now available.

OTHER USEFUL MEASURING DEVICES

D Digital vernier callipers save time and give quick, accurate results. I use this pair from Sealey Tools for everything from rim and side wall wear checks, to seatpost diameter selection, to making symmetrical handlebar tape termination points. Inexpensive and indispensable.

E A micrometer is not the most regularly used item in a cycle mechanic's toolkit but is nonetheless useful to have. Odd jobs where precise information is required about material thickness can be addressed with confidence. It does take a bit of effort to read the traditional type so anyone thinking of adding one to their collection may want to consider a digital version for ease of use.

F I was initially quite cynical about the need for a digital tyre pressure gauge but once you try one you will want it in your toolkit. This simple tool from German tyre giants Schwalbe allows you to check and fine tune tyre pressures, often putting track pump gauges to shame for accuracy. Many riders overlook the importance of using the appropriate tyre pressure for their weight and for the road conditions facing them, and this tool can make experimentation much easier. A few pounds per square inch added or taken away can dramatically alter the feel of a bike, prevent punctures and extend the service life of a tyre, so it's well worth considering.

Wheelbuilding tools

Where Allen keys and Torx bolts have simplified and streamlined the tools needed to fix a bike, wheel tools are now a very extensive and specialist area.

Basic wheel tools for servicing change with every new development in spoke and rim design. Servicing hub bearings and cassettes is now simple and fast. Where once it required the precision of a watchmaker and plenty of patience, it can now be done in minutes, albeit only with the right tools. Spoke keys are still very much a personal preference, but remember that you can do an awful lot of damage with a spoke key if you don't know what you are doing.

A Lacing wheels is not particularly complicated once you understand the process. Nipples can be difficult to manoeuvre into place, however, particularly on deep section rims or examples with single or even no eyelets. The frustration of chasing a loose nipple around a rim is something every wheel builder has experienced at some point in their life. This nifty tool allows you to load the individual nipple onto its spring-loaded mechanism and lower it into place. It is automatically ejected once the thread of the spoke is engaged.

B Correct or optimum spoke tension has traditionally been open to debate and determined by feel. Today's more exotic materials cannot tolerate such an artisan approach as the designs are fine-tuned on CAD systems with little margin for error. That is why a digital spoke tension meter has become a necessity for mechanics faced with modern wheels that need servicing or rim replacement.

C This extractor from Wheels Manufacturing is one of a set which makes bearing removal something that can be carried out effectively and with no damage to the bearing seat, ensuring the replacement will fit perfectly in its place.

D Despite recent hub design innovation there are still many on the market that need the attention of a traditional cone spanner. The Campagnolo ones are nice and thin, allowing access to most situations, and their 13 and 15mm variants are still handy for occasional brake calliper centralising.

E The Bicycle Research cranked nipple driver speeds up initial take up of spoke slack and cuts down on build time.

F It as not as easy as you may think to accurately measure spoke length. A dedicated spoke ruler is therefore an invaluable addition to the wheel builder's workshop.

G A nail punch is a useful tool to have at your disposal when spoke holes in hub flanges seem to be much tighter. A quick blow to each individual spoke head seats it tighter into the hub flange, improving its stability.

H Spoke keys are now no more standard than methods of wheel construction. Many modern factory built wheels have nipple designs that are exclusive to that particular wheel, so inevitably the spoke key count in every mechanic's workshop keeps growing. And since straight-pull aero spokes also have a tendency to twist and torque up during tensioning or adjustment, additional tools have emerged to hold the bladed section in the correct plane. Examples shown from Spokey, Sapim, Reynolds, Mavic, Fulcrum, Shimano, P&K Lie.

I Once a sealed bearing cartridge is removed from a hub—or from any other component for that matter—its replacement must be carefully installed with no unwanted pressure exerted to its inner race, as this would destroy the new bearing. Hence the need for a versatile bearing press kit like this one from Wheels Manufacturing. It comes with a multitude of adaptors and is so effortless to use I actually look forward to replacing worn out bearings.

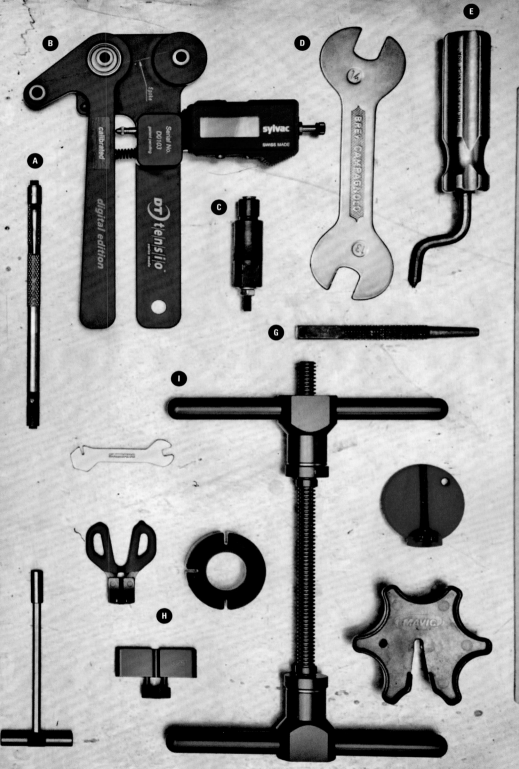

Indispensable luxury

With developments in component technology come new tools. Some old favourites keep hitting the spot, though, and luckily they are usually a one-time buy. Make sure that you have some of these in your toolbox as they save an awful lot of time, money and effort.

A A chain whip is an essential tool that is used in unison with a lockring spanner to remove cassettes sprockets from their respective hubs. This Campagnolo whip is rather beautiful.

B Traditional chainring bolts have an Allen key male part and a female counterpart with a slotted back to sandwich the chainrings to the cranks. It is quite common for the rear part to spin, so the use of a chainring bolt spanner such as this Shimano TL-FC21 makes removal and installation much easier. The widely-spaced pegs also fit some of Shimano's crank dust cap and self-extraction units.

C 'Egg cups', as they are commonly known, are used to check the alignment of the frame's fork ends and rear dropouts. They are commonly used on steel frames during manufacture or after an accident when the frame may have been bent. This particular pair from Park Tool is nicely finished and stiff enough to exert sufficient force to persuade most wayward dropouts to get in line. Use on a modern frame made of carbon fibre is for checking alignment only.

D The Shimano TL-FC16 is a dedicated tool for adjusting the preload on the firm's Hollowtech II bottom bracket system bearings. It needs to be done up finger tight to ensure that the bearings are not damaged, hence its small diameter to exert a restricted mechanical advantage.

E Campagnolo's UT-BB130 is designed to install and remove their Power Torque and Ultra Torque bottom bracket cups. It features a square drive end to allow the use of a suitable torque wrench.

F The recent flood of new bottom bracket standards has inevitably spawned a healthy growth in tool manufacture to cope with the new demands on mechanics. The removal of Campagnolo's Ultra Torque bearings is very difficult without a suitable extractor tool (see tool D on page 98) and this nicely made VAR tool works effortlessly to replace the crank bearings without damaging them.

G The cotterless crank extractor may be facing extinction but it will be a fair few years before a shop workshop can do without one. The square taper bottom bracket standard was the most popular fitting of cranks on a racing bicycle for many years. This type of tool is essential when removing cotterless cranks from their respective bottom bracket axles.

H There are several rear derailleur hanger alignment tools on the market but arguably the nicest is this version from Shimano, the TL-RD11. Any discrepancies can be addressed using a combination of care and brute force until the measurement at any point against the rim's braking surface is the same. This guarantees that the hanger is straight in every plane.

I This Cyclus Cassette lockring tool has a fitting for Campagnolo on one side and Shimano/SRAM on the other. It also has the added bonus of an integrated handle, so it saves digging around for individual tools.

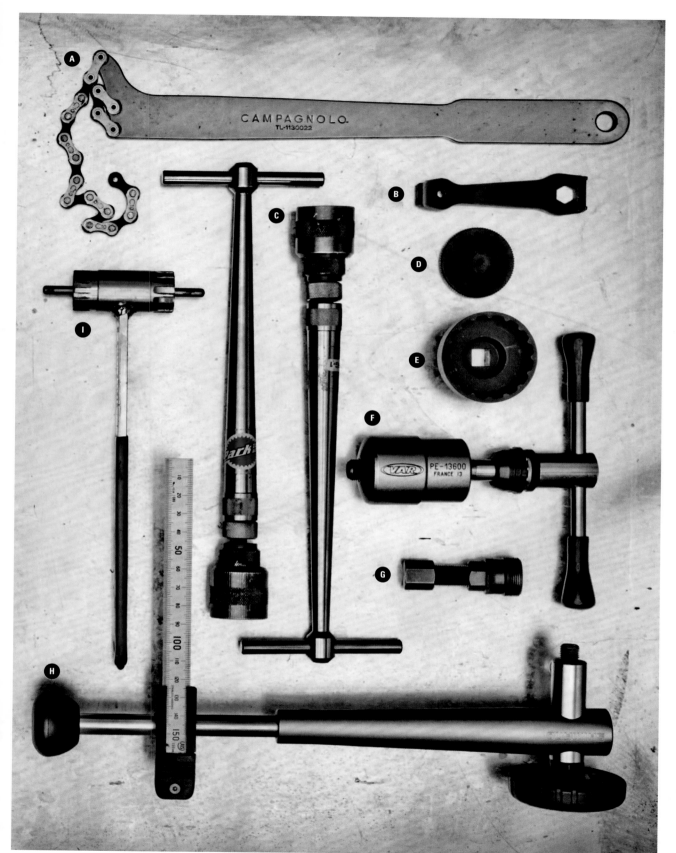

07

WORKSHOP

SÉMINAIRE
OFFICINA
WERKSTATT
WERKPLAATS

A place for everything and everything in its place

A good and solid workbench is the best investment a mechanic can make. Bench mounted vices and tools like grinders are all the better for being attached to it. Even, as shown here, when inside a team's support truck. But no matter where the workshop is, it should be a tidy, calm and well-resourced environment.

No two bicycle workshops are quite the same. Some are pristine, super-organised spaces run with a firm hand: everything has a place and everything is in its place. Others look like utter carnage yet the resident mechanic seems to know where everything lives (they may be the only one who does, however). Some workshops are run as tight as a passport control in an airport, with no unwanted bodies allowed. Others are the friendly heart of a bike shop and a social hub where copious cups of tea and coffee are consumed and the world on and off the bike put right on a daily basis.

Ideally one should aim to have the best of both worlds, making sure that the workshop is a welcoming but organised space with easily accessible tools and clear floors and work benches. Having defined areas for each type of job is sensible.

To avoid the environmental hazards that solvents create, ecologically sensitive methods for cleaning components in particular should be adopted wherever possible. New parts washer technology by companies such as RoZone—where carefully chosen bacteria eat the oily deposits—mean we are seeing an end to horribly smelly methods of cleaning and waste management. In addition, the copious numbers of cassettes and chains that an average bike shop or professional race team dumps every year should ideally be separated and recycled. It may seem like a lot of hassle but it is good practice and if everyone does their bit it can and will make a difference.

Professional teams are always on the move and these days all teams have a mobile workshop in a separate truck. It will contain all the tools they have at the team HQ, with basic power tools and some bench tools also usually included. Not to mention parts washers, jet washers and all the related cleaning gear.

Wheels and tyres are usually the main topic of conversation and debate around the truck. The choice of tyres for races is as much down to the mechanic as it is the individual rider.

In the workshop, compressors have taken over the duties when it comes to inflation and at the races they are essential. Before the compressor, young apprentice mechanics were brought along to races specifically to pump up the tyres. Even with a track pump, inflating 50 plus tyres to the correct pressure every day builds strong arms. So now a compressor does the hard part and the disconnecting hiss of a pump hose is a well-recognised sound in the race pits.

Wheels should hang on dedicated hooks, ideally plastic coated to avoid damage. Bikes should also be stored carefully to ensure that no harm comes to their paint work and anodised finishes. Space is always at a premium—the more you have the more you use—so being organised will always pay dividends.

The hanging tool board is the true sign of a busy workshop, as finding the right tool in a toolbox can be a little time consuming. Peg boards with removable hooks are a great idea, as are toolboxes with metal lined drawers. Over the years we have had the pleasure of visiting many prestigious workshops around the world and this chapter is a homage to these magical places.

**KEIRIN SCHOOL
WORKSHOPS**
Suzenji, Japan

VITTORIA TYRES
Madone, Bergamo,
Italy

CICLI PEGORETTI
Caldonazzo, Italy

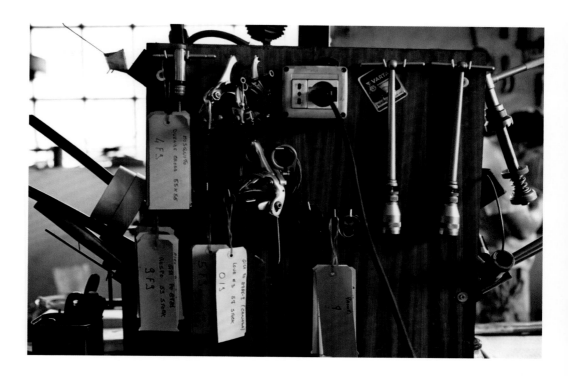

Right and overleaf:
ALBERTO AND FALIERO MASI'S WORKSHOPS
Vigorelli Stadium,
Milan, Italy

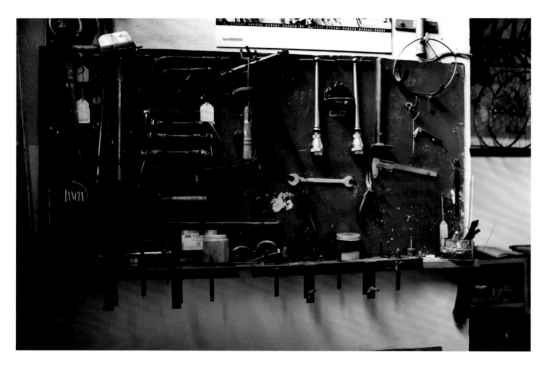

This spread:
**ALBERTO AND FALIERO
MASI'S WORKSHOPS**
Vigorelli Stadium,
Milan, Italy

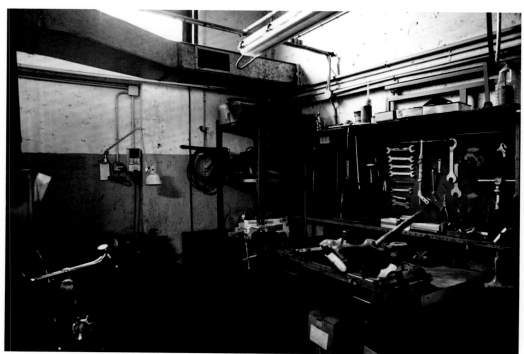

TREK
Madison, USA

MICHE
San Vendemiano,
Treviso, Italy

Right, below and overleaf:
YOSHIAKI NAGASAWA
Osaka, Japan

THE BIKE

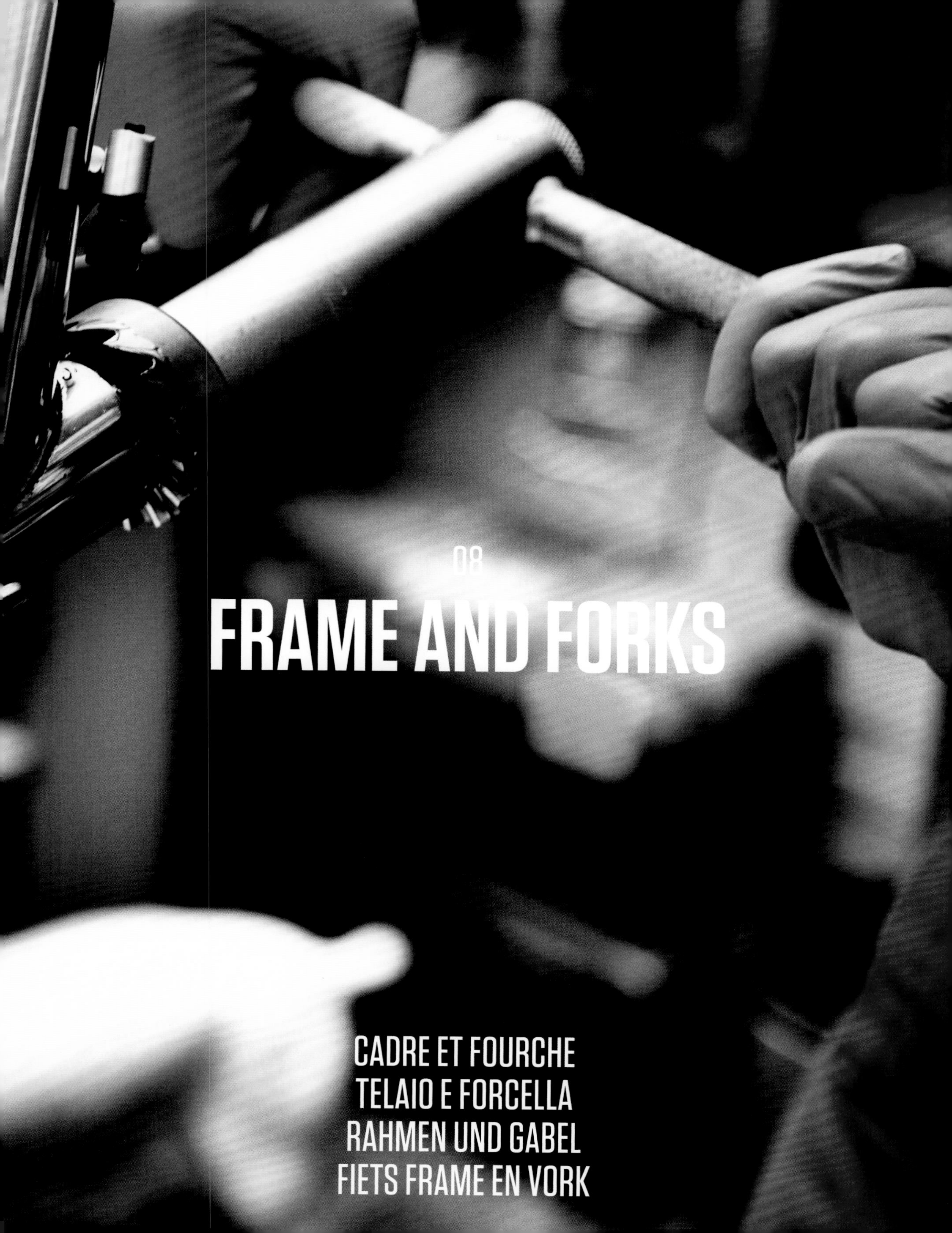

08

FRAME AND FORKS

CADRE ET FOURCHE
TELAIO E FORCELLA
RAHMEN UND GABEL
FIETS FRAME EN VORK

The frame and fork are the heart and soul of a bike

If your forks feel like they are loose, no matter how slightly, or your bikes front end rattles when ridden over poor road surfaces the headset bearings need to be adjusted. If you neglect this problem the headset wears unevenly and the bearings will need replacing much sooner. In bad cases of neglect the fork steerer can be irreparably damaged which will be potentially dangerous and even more expensive. To check this put your bike on a flat surface and apply the front brake, then rock the bike back and forwards. Any knocking or play in the headset will be apparent. Riding a bike with a loose headset will not only wear out the bearings but will also negatively affect the handling of the bike.

In some ways the bicycle frame has altered little over the last 100 years. The diamond frame and fork, when combined, still form a structure that holds the wheels at a set distance, provide locations for the points of contact and create a platform to transfer power from the pedals to the rear wheel. In other ways, things have changed a lot. Materials have come a long way and increased computing power and CAD programmes allow manufacturers to fine tune ride characteristics far more effectively than ever before.

My camera and I were visiting a celebrated framebuilder in Italy recently and, before taking any photos, I asked if there were any areas he would prefer I didn't focus on. He laughed and said to our translator that he did not mind where I looked. He threw in a culinary analogy: you can give the same ingredients to anyone but that does not mean every person will get the best from them.

The same could be said of the humble bicycle mechanic. Give the same box of bits to two people to assemble and the end results can be quite different. The differences can be subtle and hard to pinpoint but more often than not one machine will work better and just feel nicer to ride.

In all cases this will be thanks to the care and preparation during the build. Bicycle frames, new or old, should always be checked over before assembly commences. If the bike is to handle properly the headset bearings must be able to rotate freely. Too tight and the bike will wander off all over the place. Too loose and the bike will rattle over every inch of the road.

For these reasons the bearings must be precisely fitted, which means that the frame should be cut and faced before assembly commences. Any inaccuracy here will prevent the fork from turning smoothly and shorten the life of the bearings.

Each side of the bottom bracket shell benefits from being faced to ensure the cups can be tightened against clean, parallel surfaces, this is essential for bearings to run smoothly. If you wear out a lot of bottom bracket bearings the chances are you need to improve cup alignment. Although chainset design has moved on, current threaded BB shells still require good preparation to allow the bearings to turn with minimum friction.

Recent press-in BB systems have done away with the need to cut threads and face shells but I am not 100 per cent convinced that squeezing a bearing directly into a frame is a good idea. I can't help thinking that two separate cups correctly installed provides a reliable and perhaps more importantly replaceable system that leaves options open. This is not a universal opinion, however. Get 10 frame makers or designers in a room, ask them the same question and see how many different answers you get.

Seat tubes need to be clean and round with no nasty sharp edges to damage your seatpost. Bottle boss threads should be retapped if the threads appear contaminated with paint or gunk. Perhaps the most overlooked and critical aspect of frame preparation is the rear gear hanger: check it is straight and perpendicular to the rear wheel rim. Fail to do this and your gears (whether old school down tube operated, mechanical or electronic) will never work correctly.

Long story short: just because a frame came out of its box all shiny and new does not mean it is ready to start hanging parts on.

Lie all the individual headset components out and make sure you have the correct press and adapters to aid accurate installation. It very easy to damage the frame, the cups and/or the bearings if you try to improvise, so don't. Specialist tools like this headset press have been in use for many years — it's a simple yet effective method of installing head parts. Frame tools are ideally suited to the job and although initially a big investment they will pay you back. All professional mechanics will have their favourite: VAR are hard to beat.

Assuming the head tube has been cut-and-faced really all that's needed before inserting the cups is a smear of grease or assembly compound to reduce friction and ease effort required to press them fully home.

As always the devil is in the detail, so align any relevant logos or graphics, separating a bike that looks like it has been thrown together from one that has been assembled with care.

The crown race will, in most cases, need to be driven onto the fork. Some headsets use a 'split race' which means you can pop it on with your fingers.

Once the crown race is hammered home it is important to check it is seated correctly. There should be no gaps between the fork crown and the race. Any misalignment will influence the performance and the lifespan of your headset.

Slide everything into place and check there is enough clearance for a few mm of compression. A dry fit is a good idea so you can fine tune things. Once you're happy you can assemble on a more permanent basis. It is good idea to wipe down the steerer and make sure it is grease free before the spacers and stem are fitted. A thin coat of carbon assembly paste where the stem will clamp the steerer is also a good idea as it will reduce the amount of torque that is needed to hold everything firmly in place.

Assemble the forks, all the headset components, your desired spacer count and the handlebar stem. You can then measure the amount of steerer tube you need to remove.

Jot any measurements down on a Post-It note, it helps you remember if you get distracted. It also saves you going into a cold sweat when you suddenly wonder, halfway through your cut, if you are supposed to be removing 43mm or 34mm…

It is vitally important to double check any measurements before taking your saw to a fork that could be worth in excess of £500. Make sure you have allowed for the type of steerer bung you have and any compression in the bearings and, of course, the exact stem clamp depth and spacer count.

Carbon fibre dust is not good for you so it is advisable to use a mask when you cut any carbon fibre component. I use one in combination with a vacuum cleaner to extract the dust. It makes sense to use a hoover with a HEPA filter otherwise you will blow unwanted elements back into the air.

Although steel swarf is not strictly a health hazard when cutting steel steerers (see over) it is a good idea to avoid contaminating your workbench so the vacuum cleaner or trusty dustpan and brush should never be far away.

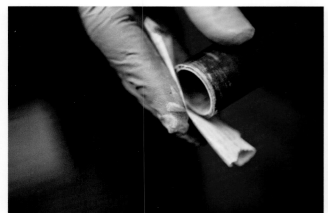

You should end up with a clean cut with no evidence of any frayed carbon fibres. Fine grit sand paper is all you really need to tidy up. Don't forget to wear a face mask.

A saw guide and carbon-specific hacksaw blade will help. Carbon-specific blades feature a rough gritty cutting edge that sands through the carbon rather than cutting the fibres. The latter can splinter the carbon and promote delamination.

Carbon fibre forks cannot be fitted with a star fangled nut so an expanding device must be used. This area of the bike is prone to the ingress of sweat which can wreak havoc on alloy parts so a smear of grease on the wedges is no bad thing.

When you apply the grease, take care not to get any on the external surfaces that need to firmly grip the internal face of the carbon steerer tube.

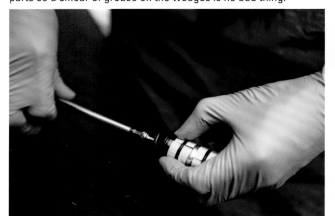
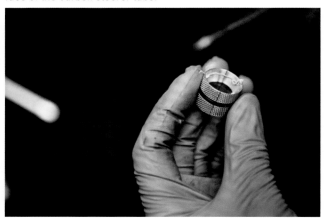

Modern ahead stems apply a fair bit of pressure to the fork steerer. As it has become the norm to remove material to save weight, the clamping surface area has been gradually reduced. This has resulted in the stem clamp working a bit like a 'cookie cutter' so extra care must be taken. I always, without fail, lightly sand the internal stem surfaces to make sure that any sharp edges are removed.

Most carbon headset spacers are not made from 100 per cent carbon fibre but rather wrap an outer layer of 3k or 1k weave around a glass fibre core. Their cut surfaces are often light grey in colour and tend to overhang the headset top cap leaving an unsightly ring. For this reason I always have a black Sharpie or marker pen on hand to colour in the offending grey ring and help it blend in better.

When installing a stem the best practice is to fit a 5mm spacer underneath the top cap. This allows the steerer to protrude further and increases the clamping area.

Lastly insert the expander bung into the steerer and attach the top cap.

If you intend to re-use a headset with another pair of forks you will need to remove the old crown race. Recent designs preclude the use of the old 'punch and hammer' technique and modern lightweight materials do not appreciate such rough handling. A dedicated fork crown race extractor that looks like a glorified pepper grinder, however, makes removal a doddle.

When cutting down steel forks a traditional hacksaw blade will suffice. Once the cut has been made, file a small chamfer on the steerer tube to remove any sharp edges and make it much easier to slide the top race into place.

A thin coat of grease helps keep everything turning smoothly. Chris King headsets don't strictly need it as their sealing is exceptionally good but an additional barrier to the ingress of dirt and water is no bad thing.

Steel forks use a device known as a star fangled nut which is used to adjust the pre-load of the headset bearings. To ensure it is positioned accurately, a star fangled nut setting tool is needed.

The star fangled nut can be loaded into the steerer using the setting tool. A hammer is used to knock it in the correct position. It should end up straight and approximately 15mm lower than the top of the fork.

Once all the individual components are in place the bearings can be pre-loaded. It is important to understand that this process only adjusts the play in the fork, so you do not need to go overboard. Final setting is best carried out when the bike is on the floor, allowing you to test for unwanted movement more effectively.

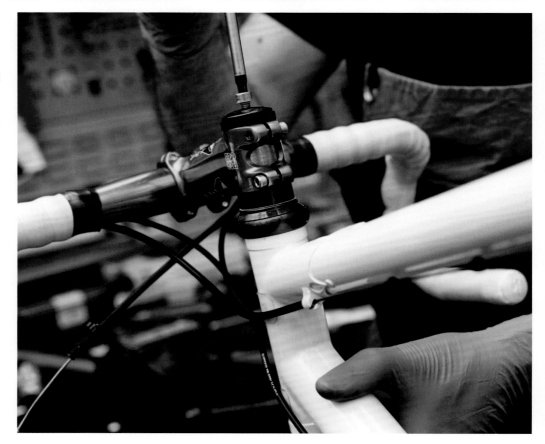

Water, dirt and impact all take their toll and eventually spoil a bike's handling and equilibrium. This Pinarello Dogma's Aheadset uses sealed cartridge bearings but they don't last forever.

It pays dividends to regularly check the condition of your headset bearings. Deterioration is slow but relentless.

If you want to make sure your bike stays creak free it's a good idea to lightly coat any mating surfaces with grease or the appropriate assembly compound. This advice particularly applies to areas prone to corrosion. In the case of the headset shown here it will make the installation process easier and less likely to cause damage to ether the bearing or the frame.

When working on the headset or removing the forks it is not necessary to completely disassemble the bars, stem and brakes. Hang the bars onto the top tube and tape them in place to prevent damaging the paintwork.

Finish Line Fiber Grip thinly coated onto the steerer before installing the stem increases grip without resorting to over tightening of the stem bolts.

Once you have your carbon forks safely back in place you need to make sure your expander bung is firmly locked down otherwise it will slip once bearing pre-load is applied. This is a common cause of rattly front ends, so make sure the adjustments you are making actually have the desired effect.

Never assume a thread is clear—any small burr, paint trace or distortion could grab the bolt and turn a simple task in to something much harder, making your life a misery. A quick run through with a tap will address any issues and allow the bolt to fit perfectly.

A spot of grease on each bolt-hole before you fit your cage of choice means that the countless drops of energy drink and sweat that accumulate will not freeze the bolt into the frame.

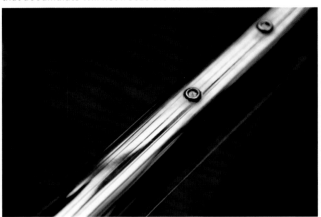

Fitting bottle cages can be a bit of a chore, especially when certain models make clear line of sight access to the bolt heads difficult. A ball ended Allen key can help, but the type with a P-shaped moulded plastic handle often end up being awkward to use. I have a pair of old screwdriver-style tools that make this potentially frustrating job a breeze.

Once you have your build underway you need to keep everything in place. One of the worst things that can happen is the bars swinging round and smacking the top tube while you are cabling up. The sound of a pair of untaped bars swinging round unchecked and making contact with a top tube will send shivers down any conscientious mechanic's spine. For this reason I tape a wad of bubble wrap or pipe lagging in place to protect the paintwork and frame.

I always add a clear film protector to the chainstay to protect the paintwork. Degrease the area thoroughly before fitting and purge any air bubble as you go. Working in low temperatures often means the adhesive won't take: a waft with a hairdryer can help.

I often run some insulation tape around the front wheel and the down tube to prevent unwanted movement during assembly, but take care not to damage any graphics on your frame. I have a huge elastic band in my workshop that does the same job.

09
BOITE DE PEDALIER

BOTTOM BRACKET
MOVIMENTO CENTRALE
INNENLAGER
TRAPAS

Preparation is the key to a trouble-free transmission

Not strictly bottom bracket-related but there are several issues that need consideration when fitting or replacing your chainrings. The first and possibly most obvious is bolt circle diameter (BCD)—not the diameter of the bolt *per se* but the distance between each bolt-hole. Smaller chainrings such as those found on compact chainsets are by default forced closer together. The 110mm BCD 'compact' is fast becoming something of an industry standard.

In the late '70s and early '80s the alloy cotterless chainset made itself known and became a differentiating feature between old 10 speeds and 'proper' racers. Square taper axles were not however the panacea to our crank and axle woes. We still had to contend with incompatible tapers, and the fact that the cheap and nasty alloys often used were prone to going on to the axle a little further every time you took one off to service the BB. Cranks often cracked where they had been greased and tightened excessively. The practice of lubricating a tapered axle and crank was—and still is—an absolute no-no as it encourages the crank to keep working loose or go on too far, in the majority of cases causing it to split and break.

Shimano's Octalink bottom bracket axle option looked set to topple the square taper's dominance. However, by holding the oversized axle prisoner inside the confines of traditional bottom bracket shell dimensions, the system's designers were forced to use very small ball bearings which were in truth not really up to the job.

ISIS was another standard that came along partly, maybe wholly, as a result of chainset manufacturers' unwillingness to license the Octalink design from Shimano. But thanks again to undersize ball bearings it was also severely compromised. While both axles were stiffer than previous styles, the bearing life was ultimately quite poor.

The arrival of Shimano's Hollowtech II system was a result of literally thinking outside the *boîte du pédalier*. A larger cup effectively extended the bottom bracket shell, allowing the use of an oversize axle together with bigger bearings, spread further apart. Campagnolo's Ultra-Torque and slightly ungainly Power Torque systems dodge patent breach yet follow a similar path.

BB development has not stopped there. The arrival of BB30 oversize axles introduced a potentially stiffer and lighter system. However, by adding another 6mm to the diameter of the axle we had well and truly run out of room inside the bottom bracket shell and so a new set of standards had to be adopted. All well and good but every time a new design emerges, frameset manufacturers are forced to revise their designs to accommodate bigger and bigger axles and bearings. Sure there are potential benefits to the structural enhancements in the bottom bracket area but it's got to stop somewhere. I often wonder how something so simple got so complicated and occasionally despair at all the systems that have come and gone, leaving a great deal of obsolete equipment in their wake.

We all want better performing bikes, but at what cost? The constant addition of new standards and product also keeps the modern bicycle mechanic on their toes. It is necessary to purchase new tools to fit and remove the new cranks and bearings as they come along.

FSA have recently tried to create a one-chainset-does-almost-all but it won't please everyone. White Industries, Miche and the latest Shimano Dura Ace incarnation, which takes both standard and compact rings, have tried to do the same. Other manufacturers have conjured up bags of plastic washers and spacers in an attempt to allow you to use a different system to the one your frame was originally intended to use.

We are going to see continuous developments in this area. Who knows: perhaps we might eventually end up with a light, stiff, reliable solution that actually lasts.

Good frame preparation is the starting point

Bottom bracket shells are another area that need approaching with care. In the old days — in other words, when building handmade steel frames — they were the next obstacle to overcome. Three thread standards existed at that time: BSA, or English as it was also known (1.370×24), Italian 36×24 and, if you were very unfortunate as it severely limited choice or the likelihood of finding one at short notice, French 35×1. Regardless of thread standard you would need to chase the threads before the cups could be safely fitted. This ensured any unwanted paint was removed and of course cleared out any unwanted spots of braze or shot, not to mention tackled any mild distortion that occurred during the brazing process.

A All threads should be checked to make sure they are clear of paint or debris and, in the case of the bottom bracket, that they are in line. Likewise faces that are destined to meet components such as cups or bearings should be prepared correctly following the manufacturer's instructions.

B Any threaded bottom bracket system should be checked before the cups are introduced. In-line taps such as these from Park Tools will clear the threads and also help correct minor imperfections.

C Facing the leading edges of the bottom bracket shell are also essential as, depending on the type of BB being used, it is advisable to ensure that the cups sit perfectly square to the frame. Attention here provides the BB with the best chance of long-term reliability. Bearings run smoothly when the bottom bracket unit goes in squarely.

D It is good practice to prep the threads with grease or an alternative assembly compound before the cups are screwed home. Finish Line's Anti-Seize is ideal and will make installation nice and easy. Perhaps more to the point, it will also make removal in several years' time a lot less stressful.

E Cleaning up frame tools takes almost as long as using them. Cutting compounds, swarf and rust on the tools will degrade the tool and prevent clean cutting the next time around. These are expensive tools and they should last a lifetime if properly looked after.

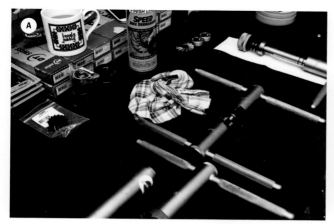

Bottom bracket cups should be torqued up to manufacturer's specification with the appropriate adapter. I have found that several tools supposedly designed for the job can damage the surfaces of the cups, so I often cover them with a bit of robust polythene that is thin enough to allow the tool to fit but offers a degree of protection.

After both Campagnolo's Ultra-Torque cups have been screwed in place the right hand crank assembly can be fitted. The bearing needs to be seated correctly so that the retaining clip can be snapped into place.

Don't forget the wave washer that compensates for variations in shell width. This should be given a coat of grease and put in the cup before the LH crank is mounted into the bottom bracket.

It is important to grease all the mating surfaces to avoid corrosion. Note the crank orientation and make sure they are diametrically opposite as it is possible to mess this up.

Unlike its steel counterparts, the titanium fastening bolt on this Super Record chainset has a left hand thread. A coat of anti-seize has been applied to prevent the threads from galling.

Campagnolo's Ultra-Torque system uses a single bolt to bring the two sub-axles together. It is located deep inside the right hand crank so an adaptor (UT-BB110) is needed to allow the 10mm Allen driver to reach inside. This bolt should be tightened to between 42–60Nm. It should also be noted that the chainset featured here is a Campagnolo Super Record Titanium variant which has a left hand thread.

The first stage in removing the drive-side bearing is to remove the small circlip. It does not have any release eyes so getting started can be quite difficult. Dexterity or an extra pair of hands can help.

Once the circlip is free then bearing extraction can commence. I use a VAR PE-13700 which draws the bearing off with ease while avoiding any chance of damage to axle or crank.

After the bearing has been successfully extracted from the axle it can be jettisoned by opening the jaws of the tool. Bearings such as these do not tolerate excessive lateral force very well so once removed they should be replaced, not cleaned and refitted.

Careful removal of the seal — don't damage the fragile lip — will allow you to double check the grease level before fitting the new units. Once the seal is removed you can either top up with Campagnolo's own LB-100 grease, or flush with a degreasing agent and allow to dry out before repacking with an alternative.

Flush and repack the replacement bearings before fitting. You only get one chance to lube them properly — as the forces required to pull them off will destroy them.

Always fit the fresh set of seals that are supplied and carefully press them into place before installing the new bearing races.

The new bearing needs to be pressed home, a task for which I used a VAR PE-13600 bearing press. Campagnolo's Ultra-Torque system features two factory fitted bearings, which will at some point require removal for replacement. They are not particularly accessible without expensive specialist tools so this is a job best left to a shop or pro mechanic.

Shimano's Hollowtech system uses a continuous 24mm axle which is permanently assembled to the RH crank. A thin coat of grease will help it slide into the bottom bracket assembly nicely.

Here we can clearly see the Chris King bottom bracket already in place. The beauty of the Hollowtech II system is that it makes aftermarket upgrades simple, so you can ditch the standard offering in favour of Chris's excellent alternative.

The splines on the left hand crank should be lightly greased to ease installation and reduce the chance of creaking under load. This process also helps when you come to strip down for servicing.

One spline is larger than all the others to help correct orientation. Remember to raise the little plastic shim that sits between the two pinch bolts before sliding the crank home, as it has a small retention pin attached that engages with a hole in the axle.

With both cranks loosely assembled on the bike, lateral play can be dialled out using a Shimano TL-FC16. This little toothed wheel is designed to lightly preload the bearing. Excessive force will introduce unwanted drag and cause premature wear.

Once you are happy with your bearing adjustment you can tighten the LH crank in place. You should nip up the opposing bolts in small incremental amounts so that each bolt applies a similar amount of pressure. The final tightening should be carried out using a torque wrench to set both bolts between 12 and 14Nm.

BB30 and 'press-fit' bottom bracket systems

BB30: The first foray with a 30mm axle diameter

BB90: Trek's oversize bearing solution for beefy frame dimensions

PF86/92: The bearings sit in an adaptor that overcomes slacker tolerances

PF30: Another solution that resorts to a small composite cups

Specialized OSBB: Used with their own crank system

BB Right: Cervelo's system with a wide bearing spacing

BB386 EVO: This system is retrofittable to virtually every BB system currently on the market through the use of a suitable adaptor

Campagnolo Over Torque: is the Italian manufacturer's attempt at a larger diameter axle with a range of adaptor cups

By the time this book is published, yet another 'new' bottom bracket bearing standard may well have hit the market. The trusty threaded bottom bracket shell has been usurped by oversize press fit systems that, whilst releasing frame designers from the restrictive shackles of the traditional BB dimensions as we know them, mean that the most important person in the chain, the end user, can be left confused.

BB30 started the ball rolling with its bigger bearings and oversized axle. The fact that many compatibility and set-up issues with these new platforms result in being forced to use adaptors, shims and spacers to make up for bottom bracket shell tolerances does irritate the purist somewhat (and I'm being polite here).

The advantages over a conventional threaded bottom bracket are that the unit is lighter (but we're only talking a few grams here) and that the bearings can be easily replaced. The disadvantages are that the bearings are often poorly sealed and wear out quickly (but because you can replace the bearings very easily this is less of an issue) and that you are limited to a few choices in crank manufacturers.

As to which system is better, there's no right answer. Manufacturers are keen to convince people that their system is better than their rivals, but the bottom line is that you can't really beat a well-prepared threaded bottom bracket shell for ease of use, compatibility and longevity.

New bottom bracket platforms allow manufacturers to beat their collective chests about reduced weight and improved rigidity, but amongst the rest of us, the question is: do we really 'need' either?

A This axle system relies on a combination of seals, spacers and washes to pack out the axle. Make sure you take note of their orientation as you remove them to ensure you refit them in the correct order. A pre-disassembly photograph will undoubtedly help here...

B Once the Left hand crank is removed the right hand crank often requires a bit of persuasion. It is important not to damage the end of the axle so a nylon-faced mallet is used to tap it out.

C BB30 bearings are press-fit so once the chainset has been removed the old bearings can be knocked out of the frame before pressing in their replacements.

D A coat of grease on the axle to ease installation and you are ready to remount the LH crank and washer.

E When dismantling the unit take some photographs of the seal and washer positions so they can be replaced in order.

F Any lateral play is taken up by a wave-shaped compression washer, which is exactly how Campagnolo's Ultra-torque adapts to any small variation in shell width.

G Large splines need a healthy amount of grease to ease their installation. BB30 axles feature a taper (unlike Shimano's Hollowtech II) so a significant amount of torque is required to force the LH crank home.

H The interface is very tight to resist pedalling forces so you will need to go all the way with the manufacturer's torque recommendation to push everything home fully...

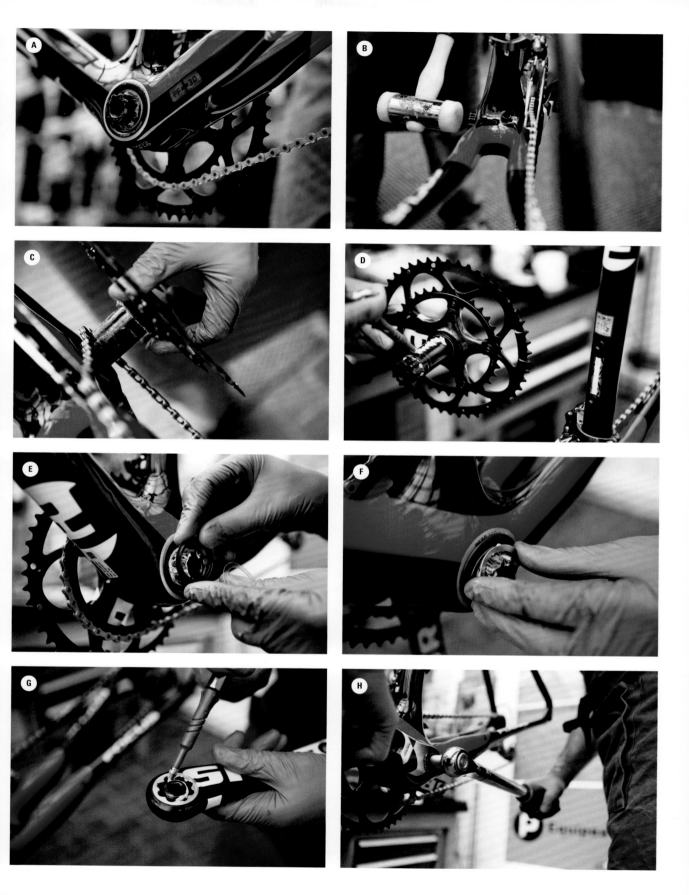

10
WHEELS

ROUES
RUOTA
RÄDER
WIELEN

Wheel choice is all down to suitability for purpose

I always struggle to understand why it's the heaviest guys who seem obsessed with weight or rather the lack of it. It stands to reason that if you are a 95kg rotund-rouleur you should perhaps not be looking at the same set of wheels as your skinny 68kg climber-clubmate. It is safe to say that anyone can complete a ride on a sturdier wheel that has a heavier rim and a few more spokes in it, because lighter wheels can easily fail and leave you stranded with a cracked rim wall, hub flange or even just a broken spoke. Sure, it won't impress the gram counters out there, but reliability and safety should always be your priority.

I still think of the spoked bicycle wheel as an engineering marvel and never take it for granted. The way the work is shared and distributed by such a frail-looking skeleton is nothing short of amazing. The front wheel must be light yet able to cope with steering and cornering forces and the rear must be able to transmit torque while coping with severe load.

The traditional 'J-bend' spoke is still in regular use and has its advantages in everyday situations and there is still something magical about a pair of hubs, rims and spokes being carefully hand-built specifically for the end user. Advances in material technology and construction techniques have without question introduced us to a new level of performance and made choosing a pair of wheels more difficult than ever. Ultimately though your tyre system choice will steer you down a specific path: tubulars, tubeless or clinchers, which will it be?

Another wheel choice that faces today's enthusiastic amateur is material. The carbon fibre rim is here to stay thanks to its ability to offer strength and in many cases incredibly low weight. When applied to tubular tyres it suffers from few major problems, especially now that special formulations of brake pads are available and adhesive that resists the high rim temperatures created during braking.

That is not to say that living with this modern wonder material is 100 per cent pain free. When a full carbon construction is applied to clincher use, the heat build-up in the thin brake pad tracks can be difficult to manage successfully. The result can be exploding inner tubes and delaminating rim walls, with inevitable consequences. Sure the pros on our TV screens can be seen using carbon rims in the mountains, but virtually every one of them will be a better bike handler than us, and riding tubulars.

In a bid to woo customers and provide safer braking there are carbon rim solutions on the market with alloy braking surfaces. One could argue that the added weight starts to negate any functional advantage, however. This is one of the reasons Mavic have, thus far, avoided all-carbon clincher rims. They offer alloy rims with what are essentially lightweight carbon fibre aerodynamic fairings. They see this as the best compromise.

For everyday use and training in adverse conditions, you probably don't really need £2,000 worth of deep section carbon. You would likely be better off with a good quality hand-built aluminium option based around quality component parts. This will allow economical repair and provide long life.

Value for money is driving the customer back to traditional wheelbuilders like Derek McLay. "I see a resurgence in hand-built wheels happening already. As the sport extends to those not previously interested in cycling, along come the heavier guys. And bigger guys demolish cheap 'off the shelf' wheels like they are going out of fashion. The wheels supplied with cheap ready-built bikes are usually of woefully poor quality — they may look the part, but that's about it. They usually have heavy rims, cheap spokes and horrible hubs with poor bearings. Luckily they are usually overbuilt, therefore when they do fail, you survive."

The quick release lever — fast and convenient

The design of the quick release lever has evolved over the years with gram saving being the main objective. Little improvement to their basic function has been forthcoming; if anything they've gotten worse. The best levers for smooth operation and feel were based on Campagnolo's original design that was facelifted several times up to around 1999 yet retained their curvaceous chrome steel lever. Close one of these and you could tackle any road surface and tear down technical descents with the utmost confidence. For some reason our friends in Vicenza changed what was nigh-on perfect to use something that although lighter simply does not have the same feel and falls short in the aesthetic stakes…

Ask a mechanic what is the most significant design innovation for racing bikes and the answer will usually be the quick release lever. Yes that's right, it may seem low tech, a small and insignificant component and something that you take for granted. But even over carbon wheels and frames, electronic shifting and 11 speed gear systems — any mechanic will tell you the iconic innovation of all time is the quick release lever because it is one of the most revolutionary innovations that cycle sport experienced in the first 50 years of its history.

Before the quick release lever you used thumb-locking wing nuts, which were slow and inefficient and became impossible to undo in the cold. And that was important because there was a time when riders received no outside help, no team mechanics and certainly no neutral support. The whole idea was you were self-sufficient. External help showed weakness in the eyes of the sport's officials extreme time punishments, disqualifications and even bans resulted from the smallest of outside intervention.

Tulio Campagnolo's system revolutionised the changing of wheels, for punctures and, in the case of rear wheels, gear changes (in those days two sprockets were featured on either side of the rear hub — a fixed wheel for climbing and a freewheel for descending). It was in 1927 on the Croce d'Aune pass during a particularly cold race that Campagnolo reached the end of his frustration with wing nuts. His hands couldn't undo the nuts and he vowed to invent a system that could be used whatever the weather. His idea was a skewer that passed through the axle of the wheel enabling a cam to close the ends tightly into the frame or fork. It remains the same to this day.

A Here in the open position the lever at the end of the skewer needs to be reset each time the front wheel is removed. The introduction of the 'lawyer's lips' rule by the UCI means that the days of rapid front wheel changes are gone forever. The initial adjustment is dialled into the threaded end of the skewer when in the open position.

B In this position the lever should start to tighten as the cam applies pressure to the fork ends and squeezes against them.

C When closing your wheel's quick release levers give some thought to their orientation and function. Do not close the levers against fork blades or seat stays in an attempt to 'neaten things up' — this just makes them difficult to open at the roadside. Wherever possible, set the front lever parallel to the ground, pointing towards the rear of the bike. This position looks best and makes wheel removal when facing the front of the bike much easier.

D It should go without saying that you need to ensure that the faces of your dropouts and the clamping areas of the QRs are grease free to ensure safe effective clamping. I have seen people try to cure an elusive creak on their bike by greasing the frame and fork where the wheels clamp. Scary — don't do it.

E Rear quick release orientation can be more tricky as the style of dropout often determines which lever positions are viable. Quick release levers should be kept clean and their pivots will benefit from light lubrication to ensure smooth operation.

Wheel changes on the road

Before rear wheel removal, open the quick release on your designated brake system and return the chain to the smallest chainring and sprocket. The tyre will then clear your brake blocks more easily, and the chain will be under the least tension so less able to put up a fight when you remove the wheel. You then know what position the chain was in when the wheel was removed so refitting will be much more straightforward.

If you have been unlucky enough to be involved in a crash, the ends of the levers are quite often damaged. I strongly advise replacing a quick release that shows any major sign of road rash because this damage could compromise your safety.

Disc brakes for road bikes are on the horizon as this book goes into publication and as such deserve a mention. Arguments amongst the *cognescenti* about the merits of this upheaval in brake, wheel and frame design that will certainly create all manner of problems in the short term and render a huge number of machines and equipment redundant in the long-term. Mike Burrows, bike design guru and seasoned racer, summed it up pretty well when he stated that, "Professional bike riders know how to ride, they don't need powerful brakes."

Compatibility issues around set-up and interchangeability, tyre grip issues, braking performance and the added headaches this will provide for race service all raise concerns. It's still too early to tell whether we will see discs adopted by the UCI and the professional peloton, but change is afoot. The debate will rage on.

A In many cases, particularly with SRAM equipped bikes, the rear mech will obscure the path the axle wants to take once the rear quick release is opened and the wheel dropped out of the frame. Practise pulling the rear mech back to clear the way. The whole process will then go more smoothly.

B Assuming you have got to grips with your rear mech and now have a wheel almost free from the back of the bike, hold the chain clear to ease the final stage of removal. Try to avoid getting the chain tangled at this point.

C Leave him to it! To make successful high speed rear wheel changes the mechanic (or in this case *soigneur*) is best left alone. A rider's intervention will only slow things down.

D Pro team mechanics always carry a set of fork and frame ends with them. These will correspond to the team's frame specification and are used to pre-setting the quick release levers on all the spare wheels. That way, they know that the wheels will fit perfectly with minimal adjustment required.

E A dummy hub is a must have for anyone who transports their bike with the wheels out or who intends to carry out chain cleaning and so they are a must have for a pro team mechanic. Not only do they help avoid the dreaded tangled chain scenario but they also help protect your paintwork and keep the chain off your car seat. Some dummy hubs come as a full rear axle so they protect your frame from compression, so ideal when packing in a bike box or bag.

Tight rear end? Frame designers can often overlook the needs of the bike mechanic. Quick wheel changes can be hampered when the rear chainstays are a bit too short and the wheel is prevented from clearing the seat tube as it is pulled from the rear drop outs. This is especially an issue as riders are now using 25mm and larger profile tubulars and tyres. Some frames even have to have the tyre deflated so the wheel can be replaced and then re-inflated in the frame. Not much use when the peloton is fast disappearing down the road…

The wheel change is a pressure situation, practice and a calm approach is essential

"Usually, in the car during quiet moments, we chat or talk by radio with the guys in the other Vittoria cars, exchanging information and commenting on the race. But that day we were all tense. It was freezing cold and the riders were racing in unbelievable conditions. We helped them to dress, to open their energy bars, to shake off the snow from their backs and shoulders. In the car the heating was set to maximum level so my hands were warm enough. And then Lastras of Movistar had a flat—I had no problems and replaced his wheel in seconds. As I pushed to get him started again, I saw his eyes: he was really overwhelmed by the effort, from the cold and from that absurd situation. I saw him again at the Giro this year and he thanked me for that help. I just remember the intense cold, the heavy snowfall and the tension of it all."

FRANCESCO VILLA, MECHANIC VITTORIA NEUTRAL SERVICE, ON THE 2013 MILAN-SAN REMO

The wheel change is the one time that a mechanic can really help his riders during a race. Good changes take a few seconds. Rear wheels and time trial bikes create another set of problems but the essential aim is always the same: to get the change done as quickly as possible.

Calmness is required to achieve this aim—not just from the mechanic, but from the affected rider. Riders know to wave for attention to the *commissaire's* car before they stop. They will hope that their team car also immediately sees the problem though either way the *commissaire* will radio to let the squad know that one of their riders has an issue. The rider will stop on the right hand side of the road, allowing all the team cars, motorbikes, press, TV and race cars to pass safely to the left.

If it's a rear wheel puncture the stricken rider will shift his chain into the smallest sprocket to enable the wheel to be removed quickly. If the team car is a way down the string of following vehicles, he will probably remove the wheel and hold it up in the air for greater visibility. If it's a team leader who is affected, the action will be even quicker: team-mates will drop behind and usually give their own wheel or even bike. This allows the leader to return to the race more quickly—and leaves the *domestique* behind to receive the service and then endure the long slog back into the race.

During the 2013 Milan-San Remo, Pablo Lastras of the Movistar squad finds himself facing a puncture. Time for the mechanics to spring into action. First of all his flatted front Campagnolo Bora wheel is quickly removed and unceremoniously dumped on the tarmac while the new wheel is fitted. The mechanic assisting Pablo presumably has to wrestle with the 'lawyer's lips' on the fork ends—the tabs

that retain the front wheel should the quick release lever come undone. In the past, many mechanics filed these tabs off to assist quick wheel changes. New legislation from the UCI intends to stamp out this practice, however. Now they have to set the quick release correctly. The result will undoubtedly be slower race service.

Once the change is done, it's time to get the stranded rider on the move as quickly as possible. A push usually helps him on his way. As well as the mechanic, the *directeur sportif* will normally have got out of the team car. That means that as one finishes up the change and picks up the wheels, the other can push the rider back up to speed. If you look closely at the picture, you can see that Pablo is in a reasonably large sprocket at the back so he can get on top of the gear quickly. If it is a rear wheel puncture, the rider will have to be pushed until he can shift into a lower gear and start pedalling.

The moment the rider is clear the car chases after mechanic Francesco, who thoughtfully collected the flatted wheel. He may have had to run 200 metres down the road to get Lastras back up to full speed.

All this takes a few minutes at most, although it still normally leaves the rider facing a long chase back to the race. Often the rider therefore calls for more service from the mechanic once back up to speed. This could be regarded as a bit of gamesmanship, as invariably there is nothing wrong with the bike, but it allows the rider to hang onto the car and get some needed assistance for the chase. The race judges will usually turn a blind eye if it's following a crash or puncture, but riders certainly can't hold on for a free ride all the way.

CASSETTE REMOVAL AND REPLACEMENT

Remove the quick release skewer before attempting to remove the cassette. The tools to carry out this procedure are relatively inexpensive and will save you time and money.

Hold the cassette firmly while attempting to undo the lockring. A chain whip is required for this and it should be wrapped around the largest sprocket before using the lockring removal tool.

Carefully remove the cassette and try to keep the sprockets and spacers in the order they came off the wheel. Once clear of the freehub body, lie them out in sequence so you know in which order to refit them.

The cassette fits onto a splined freehub body. While Shimano and SRAM use the same pattern, Campagnolo choose a deeper spline. In their defence I think the deep profile promotes better engagement. The icing on the cake is this white plastic carrier which allows all the sprockets to be transferred onto your wheel in one easy motion.

Once the sprockets are pushed fully home you can refit the lockring and tighten it to the manufacturers' recommended torque — a figure usually between 40 and 50Nm.

There is no need to load the Campagnolo sprockets individually, which saves time. Simply engage the legs of the carrier into the threaded void in which the lockring would normally reside.

The Cyclus lockring tool pictured has two sides marked HG (Shimano/SRAM) and CAMP (Campagnolo).

CARTRIDGE BEARING REPLACEMENT

This Mavic wheel needs new bearings. Each hub has a set method of disassembly. In this case two opposing Allen keys are required to undo the axle.

Once the axle is undone, the freehub can be removed — paying careful attention to the small pawls and springs which may fall out...

Once the axle is free it can be removed allowing access to the sealed bearings. If these are running rough due to normal wear and tear or the ingress of water or solvents, then they must be replaced. Most annular bearings have a serial number stamped on the outboard seal which identifies the exact dimensions and type of bearing. In rare and rather annoying cases the code number may be etched on the exterior of the bearing so it will need to be extracted first. As a general rule replace like for like.

It's important to drift the bearings out carefully to avoid damaging the seat. Here we are using an extractor from Wheels MFG that expands to grip the inner part of the bearing and allows you to use a hammer and punch to remove it safely.

Here the bearings and the extractor are being driven out using a nylon-faced hammer. I am using an old Allen key which just happens to sit nicely in the bolt head of the extractor.

After the bearings are removed and replacements sourced you are ready to press the new ones home. It is important to avoid any pressure on the inner section of the bearing. A quality bearing press such as the one from Wheels MFG is supplied with several coded adapters to suit a myriad of different bearings. Once the axle and bearings are back in situ the freehub body can be refitted. The Mavic one pictured runs on an internal Delrin bush, so cleaning up and adding a coat of very light oil to the surfaces will help keep things running smoothly.

STANDARD CUP AND CONE HUBS

Remove the QR skewer and loosen and remove one of the lock nuts using a pair of cone spanners. An axle vice protects the threads and allows you to holds the wheel securely.

Note which side each component comes from. If you are simply cleaning and regreasing, make sure that the components go back in the order that they were removed.

Every mechanic has chased rogue ball bearings across the workshop floor. To avoid this scenario I use a magnet (in this case on the end of a DT Swiss nipple locator) to extract all the loose balls in one go.

Once all the internals are removed you can clean everything and inspect the surfaces and balls for wear. If everything is in good order you are ready to regrease and reassemble.

Regreasing is a messy job. A grease gun attachment like this one from Finish Line can be screwed on to most tubes of grease, making application cleaner and quicker.

Setting the cones and locking them in place requires patience, experience and dexterity. Not too tight or too loose. They must be set just right to maintain a smooth running hub. There is something therapeutic about stripping, cleaning and rebuilding a traditional cup and cone hub. A lock nut holds the cones in their adjusted position and it takes a few years to perfect the knack of setting them just tight enough.

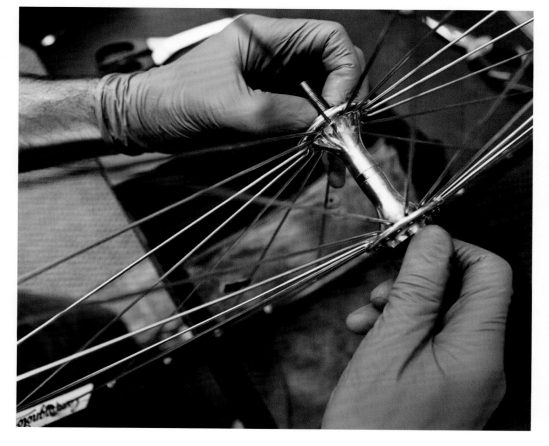

CAMPAGNOLO CUP AND CONE HUBS 1999

Campagnolo Record hubs run on the more traditional cup and cone type bearings that are, some argue, better able to resist lateral loads exerted during cornering.

The first stage of disassembly requires two 5mm Allen keys that work against each other, releasing the threaded end part of the axle.

Next, the bearing adjustment cap pinch bolt can be loosened using a 2.5mm Allen key and then removed, releasing all the other axle components.

Since they are more tolerant to lateral loads, traditional cup and cone systems arguably provide a better solution for hub bearings than their sealed siblings. Servicing a loose ball bearing hub is a bit of a labour of love to be perfectly honest. These days nearly every hub and wheel set on the market uses a sealed unit which speeds up assembly and service.

Once all the loose components have been removed they should be cleaned and inspected. If the bearing cups exhibit any sign of wear then more serious surgery will be required. Campagnolo should be applauded for making this generation of hub fully serviceable.

Popping off the rubberised seals will allow access to the resin ball retainers. Be careful not to damage them during removal, and replace them if the lips are damaged.

Make sure you get all the old grease out of the hub shell and give everything a good blast with a powerful degreasing agent before you consider reassembly.

If you lay out each individual component in the sequence you removed it and photograph them in order, you won't have to rely on memory alone when it comes to reassembly. If you have all the innards out of your hub you may as well give everything a scrub and a polish. Old T-shirts, used toothbrushes and a metal polish such as Solvol Autosol at the ready.

If you are reusing the existing bearings then it is good practice to fit the bearings back with the same cup and cone that they came out with.

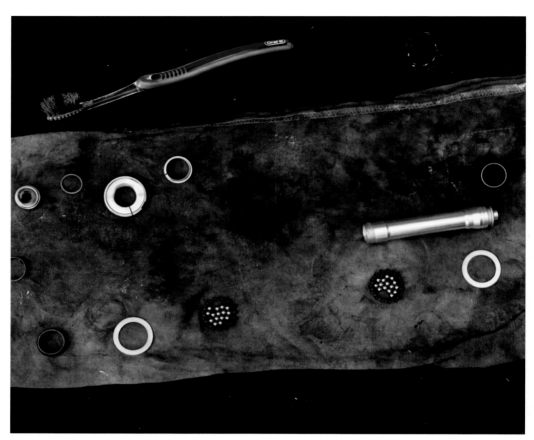

I have three key greases in my workshop that I use depending on the characteristics required. Each tube is fitted with its own dispenser to save time and reduce waste.

Once the bearings are packed with fresh grease and reassembled you can set the cone adjustment and lock everything back up. Note the small blue marker tape on one of the spokes to identify which side of the front wheel had the adjustable bearing cap on.

Over a period of use the walls of alloy and carbon clincher rims are worn away. Eventually the sidewall is no longer able to withstand the forces of a fully inflated tyre. If left unchecked you could suffer a blowout and catastrophic rim failure.

A regular visual inspection of any rim is strongly advised. As the surface is eroded it will become more and more concave. A straight edge against the rim will reveal the amount of wear. The best strategy is arguably 'if in doubt, replace it'.

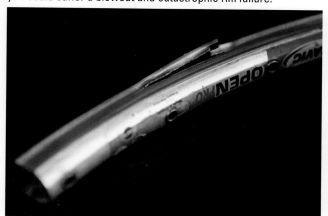

Over time, dirt oil and brake pad compound accumulate on the rim. To reduce the wear rate and ensure that your brakes perform at their best, a thorough clean every now and then is worthwhile. Mavic and SwissStop both produce abrasive blocks that can be used to clear away any contamination and get your braking back to 'good as new'. During this process any defect in the rim is more likely to come to light, so there are two reasons to do this. Some manufacturers incorporate wear indicators into the brake track of the rim, and this area of the bike should be examined regularly.

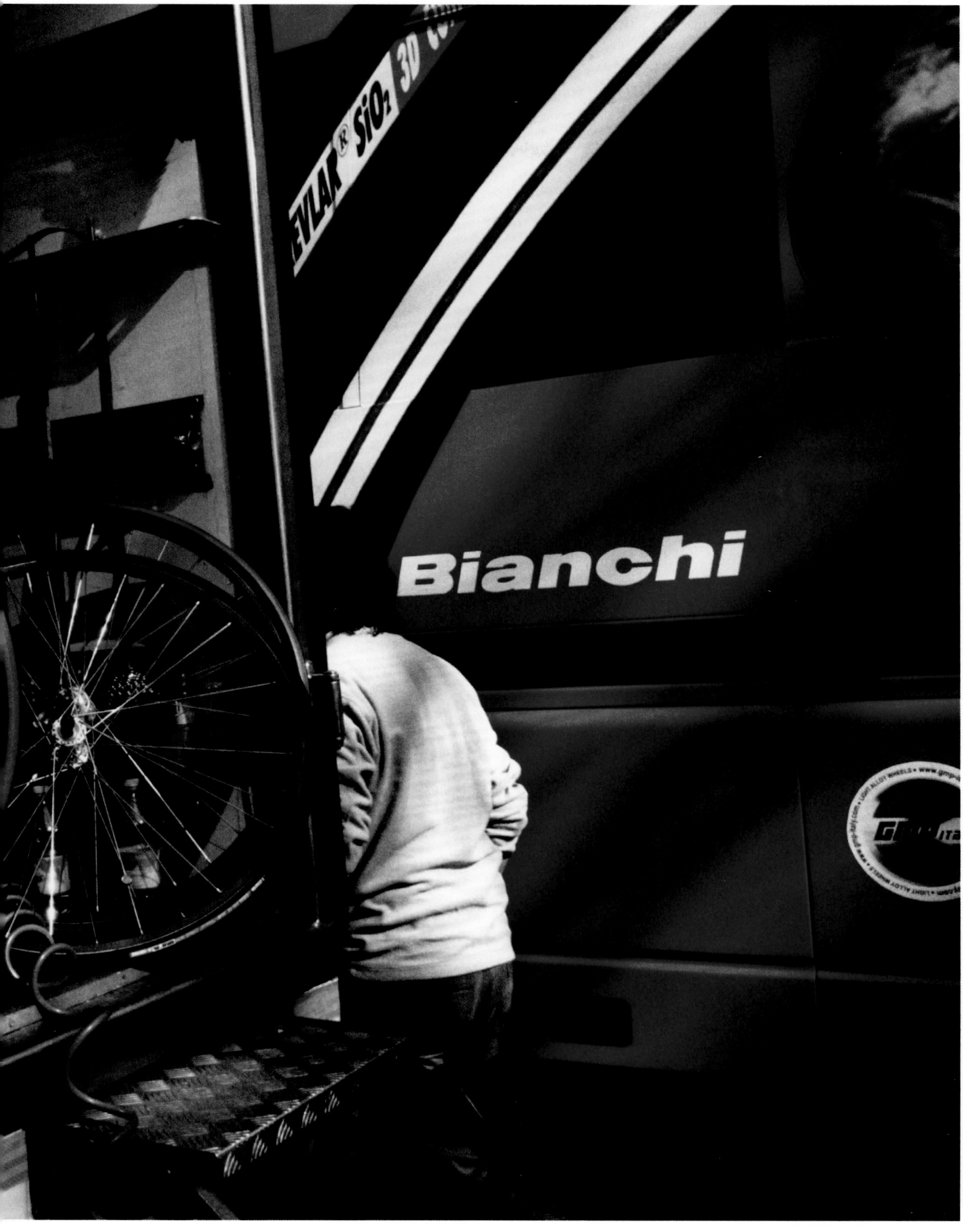
Bianchi

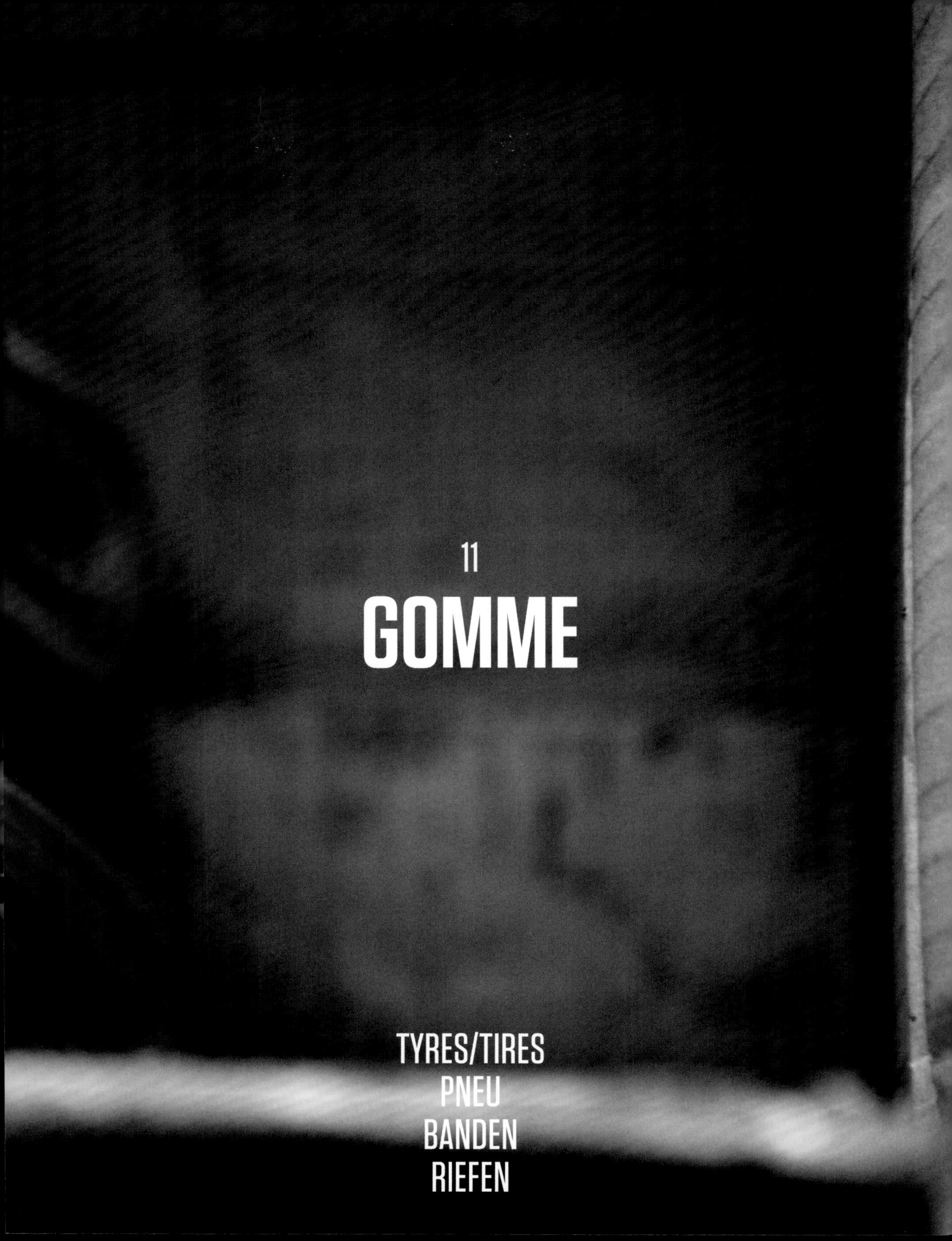

11

GOMME

TYRES/TIRES
PNEU
BANDEN
RIEFEN

Racing rubber

Tyres have a minimum and a maximum pressure rating. The upper pressure will be most appropriate for the heavier rider as it will help avoid the potential for impact or 'snake bite' punctures. If you are lucky enough to be of lighter build, though, dropping a few psi can give a more sure-footed ride and also take some of the buzz out of the road, reducing fatigue on longer rides. You should experiment with tyre pressure and consider the effect that dropping or increasing pressure has on your bike's ride characteristics.

Tyre choice is more important than you think. A renowned frame designer and carbon fibre maestro was once asked about how much could be achieved by changing seat stay material. He suggested that tyre choice and pressure could have an equal or greater influence on a bicycle's overall ride quality as the material it is made from.

The Clincher or HP (high pressure) is easily the most common tyre these days and is essentially a robust cover with a tread band of some description. The tyre is held in place by two parallel rim sidewalls with small lips that grab hold of the beads running around the inner circumference of the tyre. An inner tube is held inside and inflated to an appropriate pressure.

The tubeless tyre — not to be confused with the tubular — is a very similar animal to the clincher. However, instead of using an inner tube a special valve is mounted to the rim to make it airtight. The tyre is then filled with a liquid sealant before inflating. The advantage is that it is generally lighter and also less likely to fail due to impact. In most cases, the sealant will block any air escaping thanks to small elements such as thorns or road flints that may penetrate the outer casing. This reduces roadside repairs. The lack of a rubber tube chafing against the tyre carcass also makes for a smoother ride, something which can be quite noticeable on rougher road surfaces. The only major disadvantage is the current lack of specific tubeless road tyre and rim product on the market.

The tubular tyre is still with us despite the hassle of gluing tyres on to rims and the cost — or at the very least inconvenience — of a flat mid-ride. That said a good quality tubular is still the best way to get around: just ask anyone who has used them. They remain the number one choice of professional race teams and have a unique ride characteristic.

Developments in tyre technology mean the professional teams are now using fatter tyres in all races, not just the rough surfaced ones. The volume of air that the tyre provides is key to shock absorption because it is the only part of a bike that will truly flex. Unless there's a pivot designed into the rear end of the bike, the amount of flex in a frame and wheels is pretty minimal. If you want to get more comfortable, try a bike with a longer, smaller diameter seatpost made out of material that's strong yet flexible and resilient. Better still, an older generation saddle with a supple base material and, most notably, better padding in your shorts.

After that, it's all in the tyre. Wheels are unlikely to make a great deal of difference to the ride because they don't 'give' as much as people suggest. Heavier wheels bounce less and roll over rough surfaces and absorb the shock through their density rather than their flexibility and there are still problems in producing a larger-volume tyre: the carcass can distort and the tread becomes incrementally harder to get straight on the rim.

Grip in the wet is not particularly affected by tread design — for the most part, it is merely a placebo to help inspire confidence. The compound of rubber used provides the desired level of grip but even the stickiest of tyres cannot instil cornering confidence if they are inflated too hard. For this reason alone the pressure ratings on the tyre sidewall should not be ignored.

Puncture prevention is better than cure

We are all familiar now with Sir David Brailsford's talk of marginal gains. Attention to detail pays dividends, which is why we see one of the Sky Pro Cycling team mechanics carefully examining the tyres on this bike before the start of a TT. A small flint in the tyre could end the rider's chances before he hits the bottom of the start ramp.

In the early days of road racing, poor road surfaces meant that tread patterns and tyre width were pretty substantial. It came down to around 22mm wide in the 1960s: the proportion that seems least likely to distort under high pressure yet retain grip.

Punctures are hardly an exact science, but certain things make a huge difference — pressure (and the loss of it) being one of them. Likelihood of blowouts increases in the wet, or after a rainstorm when flints and shards of glass are washed out into the road. This is where latex tubes can help. Latex will expand further than butyl and has a suppleness that is unmatched. This is equally valid for recreational riders, as the inner tube moves underneath the tyre carcass more in clinchers than it does in a tubular. I suppose the best analogy is it's a little like acrylic compared to wool: both will keep you warm, one just feels better.

Because of its flexibility, latex also resists punctures quite well. The down side is that it loses pressure. After a seven hour stage of a Grand Tour it may have lost five to ten per cent of its original pressure. During a cobbled race

Even for time trials wider tyres are becoming increasingly popular—they are more comfortable, and provide more grip, allowing for faster cornering. Larger volume tyres also increase ground clearance, allowing the rider to pedal through corners with a reduced risk of striking the pedal on the road.

like Paris-Roubaix or the Tour of Flanders pressure loss can be up to half—though this may actually be an advantage. The earlier stages of Roubaix are run off at a blistering pace and the first few sectors of *pavé* aren't so rough. As the day progresses the sectors become longer, harder and more severe. Add in rider fatigue and the bike needs to soak up more than usual. So reaching the Carrefour de l'Arbre with only 40psi left is not unheard of and actually no bad thing. The chances of pinch flats may well be increased but the tyre won't bounce back at you, allowing riders to keep a smoother line and to change direction more easily since grip is also massively improved.

This, in short, is why handmade tubulars are still used for racing. They will withstand more abuse than clinchers. Ride and comfort is still far superior on tubular tyres and—should the worst happen—the ability to ride them flat without coming off the rim is another big plus point. On the minus side, good tubs are expensive because they are handmade, which is a long process involving skill and precision. They also require care and patience (and glue) when fitting.

Tubular tyres

The tubular tyre is made from multiple components. Fundamentally, it is a woven carcass protected by a tread band, wrapped around an inner tube and then stitched up to form a unit that can be bonded to the appropriate 'sprint' rim. It is a one piece solution, if you will, that has several major advantages over its high pressure counterpart the clincher.

Tubs are glued to a box section rim rather than relying on additional material to hold them in place. As a result, tubular rims are typically lighter than an equivalent high pressure rim. The smooth contours of the tubular rim dramatically reduce the chance of a pinch flat or snakebite puncture, which is why they fare much better when subjected to impact from stone, pothole or cobble en route to Roubaix.

Whatever the choice, historically speaking tubs would usually be bought several years in advance due to the fact that most older tyres had tread bands made from pure rubber, without modern-day additives such as silica. This meant that tyres would mature as the rubber cured, making them roll quicker and offer more resistance to punctures. Pro teams still have piles of maturing rubber at their Service Courses, waiting for the call to action. Old rims are always kept so fresh tyres can be stretched over them and lightly inflated before being put in wheel covers and tucked away in the dark from the ravages of ultraviolet rays, that can damage the threads of cotton and weaken the carcasses of the tubulars. They need to looked after like fine wine or cheese and regularly checked and turned.

Tubs might be safer in a race situation — they can be ridden flat, rarely blow out, and are less reliant on a strong rim so can be ridden when damaged by a crash — but they do puncture and create their own set of problems when they do, especially if you're just out on a training spin. So unless you have a team car following you, full of spare wheels, fixing a tubular quickly requires skill and patience and a spare tubular or some sealant... it's a messy job that's best done in a workshop and not at the side of the road. For training then, clincher tyres are far easier.

For me, the ritual of gluing new tyres was part of the appeal of racing. It was never about just chucking something on and we're done. The careful preparation and painstaking gluing on of tubs was, and still is, all part of it. The bicycle tyre is asked to respond to undulation, pothole and flint. Rain or shine, the tyre reacts to forces of acceleration and braking, cornering and sprinting. The tyre is the conduit, the communicator.

A good tyre does all these things very well; a great tyre does them better.

Fitting a tubular tyre requires care and an element of skill and patience. You need strong hands and a firm, decisive grip to get tubs to mount correctly. Over time it becomes easier, but rules need to be followed if you are to do the job successfully. But first, a few words of warning. What follows are the main stages of good tyre gluing practice — we can't guarantee the results of anything you try yourself, and poorly-stuck tubulars will roll off the rims. The results can be painful, so be warned.

Any new tubular tyre will be a tight fit on the rim (some more so than others) so pre-stretching is an essential step. Avoid the urge to place both feet inside the tyre and heave upwards as this can tear or fracture the base tape or carcass of the tyre or, worse, the stitching itself, rendering it useless. Dry mount the tyre to the rim. After the tyre is mounted, it should be inflated to its maximum pressure, left overnight at the very least, then checked to ensure it is still fully inflated and spun to check for true alignment. Dry mounting the tyre is worth practising a few times before the glue goes on, as this will give you an idea of how much finger pressure will be needed.

It sounds so obvious but do read the instructions for the glue, the tyre and the wheel. Carbon rims need specific preparation so refer to manufacturers' recommendations for guidance.

Tubular cement is really messy. Wear gloves and an apron. Clear the area of pets and children. And don't be in a hurry. You need patience and time to complete this job successfully.

Trek mechanic Roger Theel's technique for removing tubulars is certainly fast but, in the wrong hands, could be damaging. Place a big blunt screwdriver between the rim and the tyre.

Firmly grip the wheel and pull the tyre away from the rim with the screwdriver while rolling the wheel and it will come away. It does the job and, most importantly for Roger, is quick.

Glue can be thinned down. Some pro team mechanics use old *bidons* or ketchup squeezy bottles to apply it. Keep a lid on the glue though — it dries out very quickly.

Take your time. Sticking tubulars is a painful experience if you are rushing. If you allow for drying time and approach it slowly, the results will be much better.

Fitting a tubular tyre

A Before things get sticky, the old tubular tyre needs to be removed from the rim. The wheel and new tyre should be examined for defects. Rims should be clean and free of dry glue. Inspect the spoke holes and valve hole for any sharp edges — if found on an alloy rim, these should be removed with fine emery paper.

B Carbon rims are usually produced to high standards and will rarely need any form of dressing, but they should always be checked. Sanding or scoring carbon fibre is not advisable as you can easily compromise the rim's structural integrity. If you are using a deep section rim, then the appropriate valve extension will need to be fitted to the tyre, and it is important to ensure that the end result is airtight before proceeding.

C If a rim is new then it is important to ensure that it is clean and grease free. Carbon fibre rims can often be contaminated with mould release agents, so careful cleaning with a solvent — read the manufacturer's recommendations — will ensure the rim is ready to receive its first coat of glue. To make life easier, the wheel can be held in a truing stand. If you do not have one of those to hand, fitting the wheels into a bike or frame will suffice. Just be careful not to get glue all over your pride and joy. Lastly, use electrical tape to mask off the braking surface and so prevent any glue spreading onto it.

D Begin at the valve hole and carefully brush adhesive into the tyre well. Start off daubing glue at the bottom of the dip and spread evenly towards the rim's outer edge. You want to coat the whole surface of the rim but must ensure that the braking surfaces are kept free from any traces of glue. It takes a skilled and steady hand to keep the sides of the rim completely glue free — not least because most tub glue behaves like melted mozzarella — so it is usually a good idea to go around the wheel once you have come full circle. If you are happy that the rim bed is evenly covered and that your clean up is complete, the wheel should now be set aside overnight so the glue can 'go off' completely.

E Once you are happy that the tyre is ready for gluing, deflate it almost completely. It needs to be floppy but keep enough air inside to retain its shape. The base tape of most common tubular tyres is there to protect the stitching of the carcass. It is usually cotton, and in most cases very porous. Form the tyre into a figure of eight with one hand and brush on the adhesive with the other. Some base tapes are like sponges and soak up glue at an alarming rate, so it is vital that you work systematically and ensure that the whole tape is evenly coated. Try to avoid blobs and ridges of glue and work any into the base tape — the result should be a completely flat coating of glue that adds a sheen to the base tape. When the base tape sealing process has been completed, the tyre should be hung somewhere out of harm's way to cure overnight.

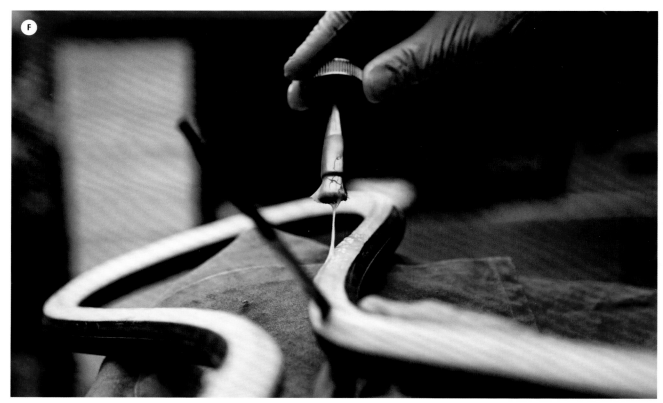

F You should now have a nicely-prepared tyre and wheel ready for the final stages of the procedure. Before we can introduce the tyre and rim together, we are going to apply a second, even coat of glue to the pre-glued rim bed. Follow the same principles as before: start at the valve hole and apply a smooth coating, making sure that no glue finds its way onto the braking surface. Continental's glue is almost completely clear, so it is important to examine the sides of the rim carefully and remove any residue before it starts to set. You then need to set aside the wheel for about 10 to 15 minutes to allow the glue to go tacky. You do not want it to go too dry, however. Monitor the rim drying—too wet and you are in for a messy job, too dry and the tyre will not stick properly, be difficult to align, and you will have to start over.

G Inflate the tyre slightly—a few psi is sufficient as you are only aiming to give the tyre some shape at this point. Any more than soft will make the tyre harder to 'pop' over the rim. Place the wheel in front of you and stand over it with the valve hole uppermost as you look down on the rim. Insert the valve into the hole while maintaining an even tension across the first few centimetres of the tub and push it down forcefully, working the tyre onto the rim bed as you go. Make sure the valve is perpendicular to the rim to avoid damaging the tyre and creating a bump.

H Maintain even tension across the first few centimetres and then bring the tyre and rim together. It is really important to keep the even pressure as you gradually work the tyre onto the rim. At this point, check that there is the same amount of base tape either side of the rim because this will prevent alignment issues later. If you lose grip, you will end up with a tyre that appears to be a smaller diameter than the rim. Do not panic if this happens—just pull the tyre away gently and start again applying more force and try again.

I If the tyre was properly pre-stretched, you should not have too much difficulty making good progress as you reach the final stage of pushing the tyre over the lip. Ensure that you keep it as straight and close to the tyre's final orientation as possible. You do not want to roll the tyre over the lip of the rim as you go—instead, lift it into place. You will end up with glue all over the tyre sidewall otherwise, and it's really hard to get off once it's on. The last few centimetres are always the hardest. An additional pair of hands at this stage can come in very useful, even for the most experienced mechanic.

J Once the tyre is seated into the rim you need to quickly check that the tyre is centred: this requires strong fingers and fast work.

There are two accepted ways of sticking a tubular to a rim—tape or glue. In common with most professional team mechanics, I prefer glue, which is the technique we cover here. Over the years I have tried many brands of adhesive but German tyre giant Continental makes consistently reliable, quality products suitable for both carbon and aluminium rims.

Patience when gluing tubular tyres is even more important than skill and technique. Take a seat and allow yourself time to spread the glue evenly. If you enjoy the process it will be successful. Rush it and you will almost certainly end up with more glue on you than on the tyres.

K Now inflate the tyre to maximum pressure. Providing you have not allowed the glue to dry out too much, the tyre will—in 99 per cent of cases—do most of the self-righting for you. If the tyre is terribly wobbly, it may be better to pull it from the rim and start again after adding an extra layer of glue to the rim bed. You will find that the extra glue soon 'melts' into the previous layer, allowing it to be smoothed over. If the base tape has lost some of the glue you carefully applied the day before, it may be necessary to apply some more. As long as you have only lost a bit here and there you do not need to leave the touched-in areas overnight before tackling again.

L Once fully inflated, spin the wheel and check the tyre for any deviations. If you find any, simply grip the tyre securely and force into alignment. If it is very difficult to move, try lifting the tyre vertically and lowering into place. Spin again and check again.

M Once you are happy with the accuracy of the tyre fit, you need to ensure that tyre and rim are well stuck and that any air bubbles and gaps are dealt with. First, roll the wheel across the floor while gripping the axle firmly and exerting strong pressure to make the tyre sit deep into the rim well. If you are using a bike as a workstation, you can then sit on it and roll forwards and backwards carefully to ensure good adhesion. Then grip the wheel firmly and push down at an angle to the floor, as if the wheel were banked over cornering. Press hard, release, turn the wheel a few degrees and repeat. Work all the way around the circumference of the wheel and then, when happy, flip the wheel around and repeat on the other side. Once this is done, you should have a tyre that makes full contact with the rim and is well stuck and true.

N Before you break out the rim cement, insulation tape can be applied to your rim's braking surface to prevent contamination during the preparation and tyre fitting stages. This tape 'barrier' will significantly reduce clean-up time if glue oozes out from between the tyre and rim bed or has been accidentally smeared onto the rim during the gluing process. Once you're all done and happy with the results the tape should be carefully peeled away and the rim wiped down with a lint-free cloth dipped in a degreasing agent to ensure all traces of tape adhesive are removed. Leave the wheel overnight to ensure maximum adhesion and then check the integrity of your work the following day by rolling the tyre from side to side. Happy with the results? Then you are ready to roll. If not, well, you know what's coming next—I am afraid the whole lot needs to come apart and you need to start again. Depending on the condition and amount of glue on the tyre and rim it may need regluing and setting aside before attempting again.

Clincher tyres

The tubular tyre now tends to be the preserve of the committed racing cyclist. Most of us now choose to use high pressure clincher tyres — cheaper, easier to repair, and generally more convenient. Some even argue that recent developments have seen the clincher edge ahead in pure performance terms. Even the early adopters of tubeless systems are admitting that the tubular tyre's well documented comfort advantage could be challenged. We are certainly spoilt for choice when it comes to tyre selection with major manufacturers like Continental, Vittoria, Michelin and Hutchinson all turning out great products.

Despite all the options available you should be able to narrow them down fairly quickly. The type of riding you are doing, the road surfaces you are likely to encounter and your physiology all help refine your tyre choice. Heavier riders frequenting the Surrey lanes or the cobbled climbs of the Ardennes should not be looking at the same tyre as a triathlete who weighs 60kg when soaking wet.

Weight is not the only thing you need to consider when choosing a tyre, however. The volume of a tyre can also have unexpected benefits on poor road surfaces and dropping the pressure a tad can help smooth out some miserable road surfaces more than a bendy carbon fibre seat stay ever could.

Some tyre manufacturers incorporate patterns into the tread but I am reliably informed that it is the compound of the rubber rather than the surface detail that influences a tyre's wet weather performance. I have tried a fair few tyres over the years and settled on a handful that I like the characteristics of. Everyone is as different in the conditions in which they ride, so it is worth experimenting.

When fitting a new tyre, remove the old one, the tube and, if necessary, the rim tape. Since many modern tyres are intended to be fitted in a specific direction of rotation, first check your tyre sidewall for orientation information. While the sipes (indentations and channels) in the tread of most road bike tyres are largely superficial, it is quite likely that the tread has been laid a certain way or that the tyre carcass is woven in a pattern that is happier rolling one way rather than the other.

If your rim has spoke holes, check that your rim tape covers all of them. Rim tapes are generally plastic, self-adhesive cloth, or rubber. There are also hybrid tapes on the market. I favour these as they are reusable, resistant to high pressures and do not absorb water. That makes them less likely to suffer from water retention or encourage internal corrosion. Make sure any tape is in good condition, covering all sharp edges and protrusions.

Of course, recent developments in tubeless wheel technology have resulted in new styles of rim that do not have traditional spoke holes, so rim tapes are becoming less of necessity.

Hang the tyre over one side of the rim, taking note of any directional requirements (arrows on the sidewalls). While you are at it, line the graphics up with the valve. Not only does this avoid you dropping valuable style points but it will assist you in tracing an offending article — like a shard of glass, a thorn or a flint — if you puncture.

A coat of talcum powder helps the tube to move freely inside the tyre and potentially reduces punctures as a result. Coating with talc also eases the installation of your tyre.

To avoid wasting talc and getting it all over the place, leave the sprinkler holes closed and drill one 2mm hole in the middle of the cap. This allows for more accurate dosing.

Fitting a clincher tyre

When selecting your inner tube, make sure it covers the size of your tyre comfortably. If you use the most common 23mm section then an 18–25mm tube will be fine. They often cover a reasonable range of options, but a tube that is too wide will be difficult to persuade to fit and a tube that is stretched to the limit will be more likely to suffer from punctures. Make sure that the valve is long enough for your chosen rim profile. Too long is functionally acceptable but too short is useless.

A Inflate your tube lightly, just enough to give it some shape with no creases or folds, and then seal the valve. Place the valve through the hole in the rim and start feeding the tyre into the rim bed. There are heated arguments in many shops about which way to approach fitting. To start at the valve or to finish at the valve, that is the question. I advocate the first method. This allows you to depress the valve slightly and then tuck it away. I use talcum powder inside the tyre casing. This helps the tube move easily inside the casing which is good for two reasons, firstly it assists the installation of the tyre and secondly it enables the tube to 'move' very slightly as it is inflated, preventing high spots or twists in the tyre as it reaches maximum pressure. There is also an argument that says that it can help in puncture prevention, as this movement assists the tube's flexibility — either way it makes the job much easier. Once talced up slip the lightly inflated tube into the open side of the casing and then tuck away into the rim well so that no part of the tube protrudes.

B I always set off at the valve and get the first few cm in place before pressing the valve stem up inside the rim until the bead of your tyre drops into place. This way you know that the valve seat is not trapped and taking up valuable bead circumference. Work the tyre symmetrically round the rim using force to stretch the tyre towards your final destination diametrically opposite the valve. Pay careful attention to the graphics on your tyre of choice and align a letter or an element of the design with the valve stem. Not only does this look smarter and show an attention to detail but functionally it creates a reference point should you suffer a penetration puncture which will assist with the location of the puncture and the removal (if required) of the cause...

C Most tyres can be eased over the rim. Follow the tyre symmetrically and equally around the rim — stretching towards the floor will ease the final snap over the rim. Sure, there are some combinations that are thumb blisteringly tight but resorting to a set of tyre levers (or, heaven forbid, spoons) will almost certainly result in a trapped inner tube. It takes a fair bit of practice but, if you remember to apply talc and to only lightly inflate the tube initially, you should be able to do it. It might be a struggle, but being methodical gets the job done. The last bit is always tricky but if you have the right amount of air in the tube, have added talcum powder and worked the bead into the well of the rim, you should be home free.

D Once you get to the last few centimetres you will need to lift the bead over the rim using your thumbs. Avoid the temptation to use a lever or any other implement as you will most likely damage the tube and possibly the tyre and rim. Don't give up too easily, if the tyre is simply 'too tight' back off a bit and re-work the tyre, stretching it slightly more forcibly to steal a few more millimetres, which is often all will take to snap it over the rim edge. It's 95 per cent technique and 5 per cent brute force but you should never really resort to using tyre levers to mount a tyre to your rim.

E When your tyre has finally snapped into place you should undo the presta valve and add another 0.5 bar or so then lock it back up before starting at the valve and checking that you have no section of the tube trapped between the bead of the tyre and the rim. If you fail to carry out this step you can end up with a spectacular explosion as the tube fails during inflation! When the tyre is soft you can also massage the tyre into place at this point so that it sits correctly with no unwanted wiggles or high spots. Only then should you finish off the inflation process. This method helps eliminate the eardrum bursting sound of a tube which has been trapped and left unchecked before being fully inflated.

F Check the sidewall of your tyre to find its recommended pressure range. All tyres will have a minimum and maximum that should be respected. Heavier riders should run near or at the highest pressure suggested and the lighter user is best working towards the lower figure. Tyre pressure can dramatically affect the ride quality of your bike so it worth experimenting. In wet cold conditions dropping a few psi can significantly improve traction and safety. Assuming you have decided on the appropriate pressure for you personally all you need to do is get pumping. A high quality track pump with a large easy-to-read gauge is an absolute must have so make sure you invest wisely. Consider material, dial legibility, hose length and valve chuck design when making a purchase. Give the wheel a quick spin to check the tyre is running true and seated correctly and you're ready to roll. If the tyre is out of true, deflate to about 2 bar and try to reseat before inflating to pressure and checking again. Don't underestimate the importance of running the correct tyre pressures. The manufacturer knows best, so don't be tempted to stick in a bit more than their suggested maximum for luck. Generally the highest rating is aimed at heavier riders and ideal road conditions. Experimentation is the only easy way to find out what works, and a small digital pressure gauge like the one in the picture makes 'bleeding' a tyre much easier. Use a pressure gauge and check your tyre pressures before every ride.

Steel beaded tyres are much easier to work with (but heavier) as their steel beads hold their shape but some folding tyres with Kevlar beads need a bit more effort to coerce into place.

12

BRAKES

FREINS
FRENI
BREMSEN
REMMEN

Braking power is all about regular servicing

Cable health has a massive impact on the efficiency of your braking and of course on gear shifting performance. Overlooking cable replacement when servicing is common, but really is a false economy. If you use a bike regularly in all weathers, chances are two seasons is all you'll get before cable performance starts to suffer. This is particularly notable on bikes with tight cable bends or torturous paths for the cables to negotiate. When fitting new cables ensure that you leave enough length for the handlebars to turn fully left and right without restriction.

Despite all of our attempts to propel the bike as quickly and as efficiently as possible, at some point you are going to need to slow down, regulate your speed or simply stop. The humble rim brake is a crude mechanism but much has been done to improve its performance in recent years.

There are obvious arguments for disc brakes on a road bike. As well as being reliable in all weathers, they eliminate braking surface wear and so consign worn rim wall blowouts to history. Hydraulic systems also do away with cable friction, allowing smooth, consistent long-term operation and place less importance on cable routing — potentially opening up more creative paths for frame design.

Even so, they currently add weight and require every frame manufacturer to go back to the drawing board. Anchor points on lightweight carbon frames in particular will have to be designed very carefully and almost certainly have material added, again increasing weight and potentially adversely affecting the ride quality into the bargain.

So right now a well-set up, high quality brake calliper is as good as it gets. The dual pivot design dominates the marketplace, though Campagnolo for one offers a more traditional single pivot rear option on several of their upper end brake sets. This allows you to decide how much rear braking force you want. Heavier riders tend to need a bit more but since the majority of the braking is performed by the front calliper, it is not perhaps quite as critical as it may seem. For many users, it is therefore just an opportunity to shed a few grams. Most other manufacturers' models have this differential braking force requirement built into their design to reduce the chance of locking the rear wheel if you are a touch overzealous when slowing down.

Another reason to question the disc brake's introduction — how good do your brakes need to be on a road bike?

No matter what brand or style of brake calliper you have, there are some basics that need to be taken into account if you are to achieve braking perfection. First I suppose is whether your brakes actually fit the frame correctly and whether the pads are able to fully engage with the rim's braking surface. If your brake calliper is too shallow than it may not reach the rim. Likewise if it is too deep it may not allow correct pad alignment.

Good braking performance is also reliant on all the pivots of each calliper moving freely. This makes regular cleaning and lubrication of all the pivots essential, together with occasional brake cable checks to ensure the inner wires pass smoothly through the routers with no noticeable drag. If your bike has a couple of seasons behind it, then replacement of the brake cables is probably overdue. Don't be tempted to just fit new inner wires. It is a false economy: inner wires are made from steel whereas the liners of the outer are plastic. It's obvious which one is going to wear out. Replace the job lot occasionally and enjoy the same level of braking performance you had on day one.

Other tips include keeping your rims and pads clean, digging out with a small pick any debris that is trapped in the pad material, monitoring brake pad wear and keeping an eye on brake lever travel, making appropriate adjustments where necessary.

Mounting brake callipers is less straightforward these days, with many frames and forks requiring alternative mounting nuts to provide a safe fixing. You should always take great care to use a nut that provides the maximum thread engagement.

Brake pad replacement should be undertaken with care. It is critical to fit the new blocks correctly, noting their orientation and also their compound. Always follow wheel or rim manufacturer guidelines.

The next issue is to ensure you have the correct brake pad for your rim type if you have swapped wheels. Carbon damages easily if alloy rim specific pads are used.

Carefully select your brake pad compound and make sure that the pads do not overhang the rim's brake track. If you run two or more pairs of wheels of differing materials in the same bike, you will need to change the blocks every time you swap your wheels over.

Precise brake pad alignment is vitally important and some rims have a generous braking surface but others less so. Don't assume the pads will need to be in the same place if you swap out your wheels.

When cabling up, manage the exact path each housing will take, keep unwanted friction to a minimum and also provide sufficient length to allow the bars to turn fully both left and right.

Most quality brake and gear cable housing will feature some graphic or other. Where the logos end up really makes a difference to the aesthetic of any bike.

Use a bench mounted grinder to dress the ends of the cables once they have been cut to length. Grinding them flat means that they are a better fit into the ferrules and less likely to hinder the inner wires.

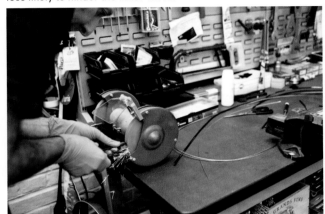

Brake cable housing will be damaged or distorted after trimming to length so it's good practice to tidy up the ends using a bench grinder or a decent file. Don't get too carried away, though: the heat created can melt the low friction liner found in nearly all modern cables.

One of the most cherished items in my workshop is this old tool that I discovered in my grandfather's garage many years ago. I straightened the end of it out and use it to open out the lining of outer casings that gets compressed during the cutting process.

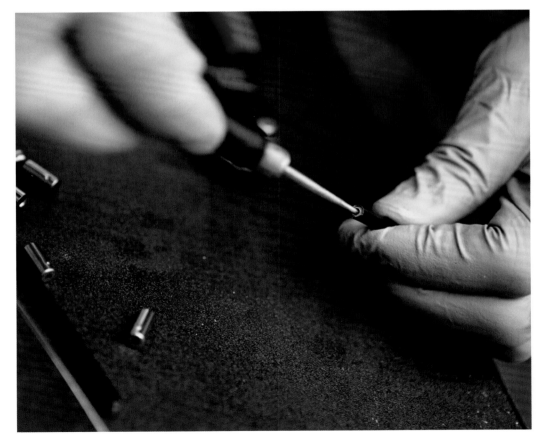

Brake centralisation is an often overlooked and misunderstood area of brake setup. It is critical to attend to this if you want to get the very best performance out of your brakes and to, of course, avoid unwanted rim rub when climbing or sprinting. Most quality brakes have small, integrated adjusters incorporated into their design. You should aim to get your brake pretty close in the first stage of installation though: adjusters should really only be used to fine tune things.

Outer casing should always be terminated with the correct specification end-cap (if one is needed). Note that gear and brake cable outer casings are different diameters.

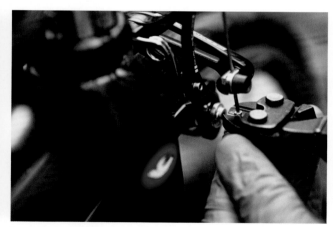

Inner wires should be cut to length and terminated with an alloy end cap. They should all match and be neatly crimped... frayed cables not only look shabby but they're also very sharp.

13

DRIVETRAIN

TRANSMISSION
TRASMISSIONE
GETRIEBE
TRANSMISSIE

Neglect will cost you watts as well as money

A knock in transit can easily disturb a modern replaceable gear hanger. It only takes a minute or two to check and to correct any discrepancy.

This park gear hanger alignment tool assists in the correction of any misalignment of the rear gear hanger. Neglect this critical area and your indexed gears will never work at their best. To shift a chain faultlessly from sprocket to sprocket requires several parameters to be met but the first is for the rear hanger to be straight and perpendicular to the wheel. There are several tools on the market that allow you check and correct any issues. Even brand new frames may need checking and adjustment to get them within tolerances.

Modern indexed drivetrains with 9, 10 and now 11 sprockets require precise adjustment to get the best out of them. Although the more adventurous home mechanic may know better, it is generally accepted that the only way to guarantee your high performance derailleur system works as intended is to work with compatible components. Each manufacturer has their own idea about the ideal specification for their products. Adhering to some golden rules during installation will avoid poor operation, injury and even death if the instruction manuals are to be believed.

It is unwise to start trying to be clever and mix 10 speed parts with 11 speed. It can work but often by mixing components you will never get all your adjustments spot on and end up with shifting issues and probably some unwanted chain rub into the bargain.

Cable housing length and routing need to be carefully monitored to avoid unwanted friction at any point. Just as with brake cables, gear cable outer casing will deteriorate over time so seasonal replacement is advisable. You will be amazed at how much shifting performance drops off without you noticing: the friction builds up very gradually, placing unwanted strain on the shifters that can often contribute to premature failure. If your shift levers feel stiffer in operation than they used to, do not ignore it. The results of doing so can be expensive.

On a modern racing bike, chain wear is perhaps the most important aspect of drivetrain health to monitor. Thanks to the space constraints caused by squeezing so many sprockets into such a small space, chains have got thinner and thinner. That has made them lighter, which is great. It has also considerably shortened their lifespan—not so great. A normal lifespan for a quality 10 or 11 speed chain is now seen as around 3,000km. Many moons ago a trusty Sedisport running on six or seven sprockets could see you through a whole season... or even two.

A laser-cut chain wear checker is an essential addition to anyone's toolkit. Even if you do not have the skill or confidence to replace your chain you can at least check it for signs of excessive elongation. Most of the commercially available tools are calibrated for 0.075 and 0.1mm stretch detection. If you catch the chain at the first measurement you may well avoid the scenario where other drivetrain components reject a new chain.

Once this window of opportunity is lost and 0.1mm stretch is exceeded you will almost invariably have to replace the cassette and if you really have ignored the health of your chain, your chainrings may also be in danger.

There are some basic stages to fitting any chain and a dedicated tool will often be required to complete the task successfully. Assuming that you have caught chain wear early enough that you can continue to run the same cassette, make sure the replacement chain is compatible. If you are going to keep all the other transmission components, remove and clean them so as to avoid contaminating the new chain.

If you are confident that your existing chain is the correct length you can use it as a guide when cutting the new one to size. If you are changing your cassette gear ratio or altering chainring sizes you will need to start from scratch. Also remember to follow any directional information: several chains can only be run one way. The three main transmission manufacturers have specific methods of determining the optimum chain length, so be sure to follow their advice.

These rear end alignment tools have become something of a workshop rarity in recent years. Affectionately known as egg cups, they were regularly used to correct any misalignment of dropouts on steel frames, a common cause of broken rear axles. Once installed the faces should be parallel. If they are not, manual manipulation is required to bend the offending dropout into place. Not a good idea on modern carbon frames but handy to check the frame for imperfections before you start the build.

The very first thing that should be established is whether the rear derailleur hanger is aligned correctly. This is a common cause of indexing problems.

Once the tool is screwed home, in place of your rear mech, several reference points can be accurately measured against a true rear wheel.

Most chains come out of the box with an excess of lube applied. This will inevitably attract dirt if left unchecked. It's worth spraying a bit of degreaser on a rag and giving it a quick wipe before fitting.

Make sure you invest in a quality chain tool to ensure any work you carry out doesn't compromise the integrity of the links. There are some exotic models on the market but this reasonably priced model from BBB works well enough if your budget is tight.

SRAM were one of the first to introduce a 'Power Link' that allows you to make or break your chain without the need to tamper with the rivets. They do however appear to stretch slightly quicker than the normal chain links, so wear should be monitored regularly. These Power Links can be difficult to open after they have covered several hundred kilometres, but there are inexpensive tools on the market from manufacturers including Park, KMC and BBB that make the task much easier.

Care should be taken when tightening the band on front mech clips. Steel carbon or alloy tubes need to be treated with equal respect as they are all susceptible to damage if you are over-zealous with your Allen key. I use a light coat of Finish Line Fiber grip paste on the inner surfaces of the clip to reduce the amount of pressure required to keep the front mech firmly in position.

Most front mechs come with a little adhesive label to assist initial positioning above the outer chainring. Between one and three millimetres is normally sufficient to provide clean shifts.

Before fitting the chain, it is worth checking the upper and lower travel screws. This prevents overshifts and potential damage to the crank or frame later on in the set up procedure.

The upper travel screw should be set using the jockey wheels and top (smallest) sprocket as a reference. If anything I set it conservatively to protect the frame from potential damage, and let it out carefully once the chain is fitted.

Lower travel screw setting could be considered even more important since, if you forget to limit the travel, a destroyed rear wheel is quite likely. Again I restrict the inwards travel slightly and fine tune once the chain is on.

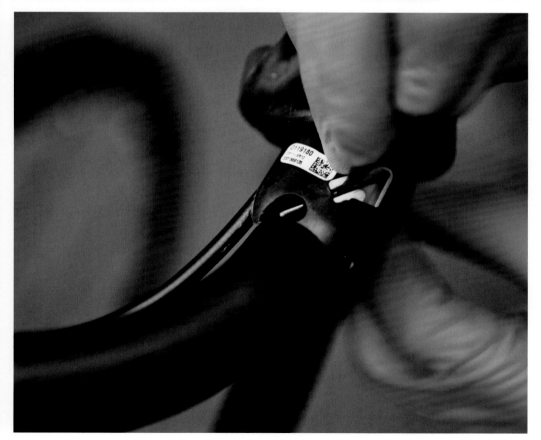

Campagnolo's Ergopower levers provide dual cable routing options, as do offerings from SRAM and Shimano. Your bar shape and chosen lever position tend to favour one routing path over another. It is very important not to kink the inner wire when feeding it through the passage in the lever body: any deformation will result in an undesirable increase in friction which will ultimately hamper precise gear shifting.

It's a good idea to bed the cable by stretching a few times once it's clamped. Then release it and set it correctly. It's also good practice to turn the rear adjuster anti-clockwise one and a half turns before clamping it again. That way you can adjust the cable tension until it is set perfectly. The biggest problem with internal cabled bikes is that you cannot easily get hold of the inners and give them a good tug, so the bedding in process can be a bit long winded.

A firm pull with some decent quality pliers will take up most of the slack.

I don't know why some people make such a mess of terminating inner wires — that's if they bother to do it at all… Leave a short length before fixing a cap with a neat double crimp.

Once the bike is complete you can get stuck into the final stages of adjustment and setup. I run though the gear operation repeatedly to bed in the cables and housings.

Time taken to get the adjustments spot on will ensure reliable operation out on the road. Sometimes the smallest of tweaks can make a difference, but make sure you get all that cable stretch out before you head out of the door.

A dropped chain is at best inconvenient and, at worst, catastrophic for paintwork, so install a chain catcher, regardless of how well adjusted a front mech appears to be. Modern carbon fibre frame designs usually require a device that bolts to the front mech. This titanium and carbon frame from Independent Fabrication uses elegant lugs which accommodate this simple Dog Fang from Deda. You just put the bike in bottom gear (big at the back, small at the front) and set up one millimetre away from the inner face of the chain. Simple, cheap, light and effective.

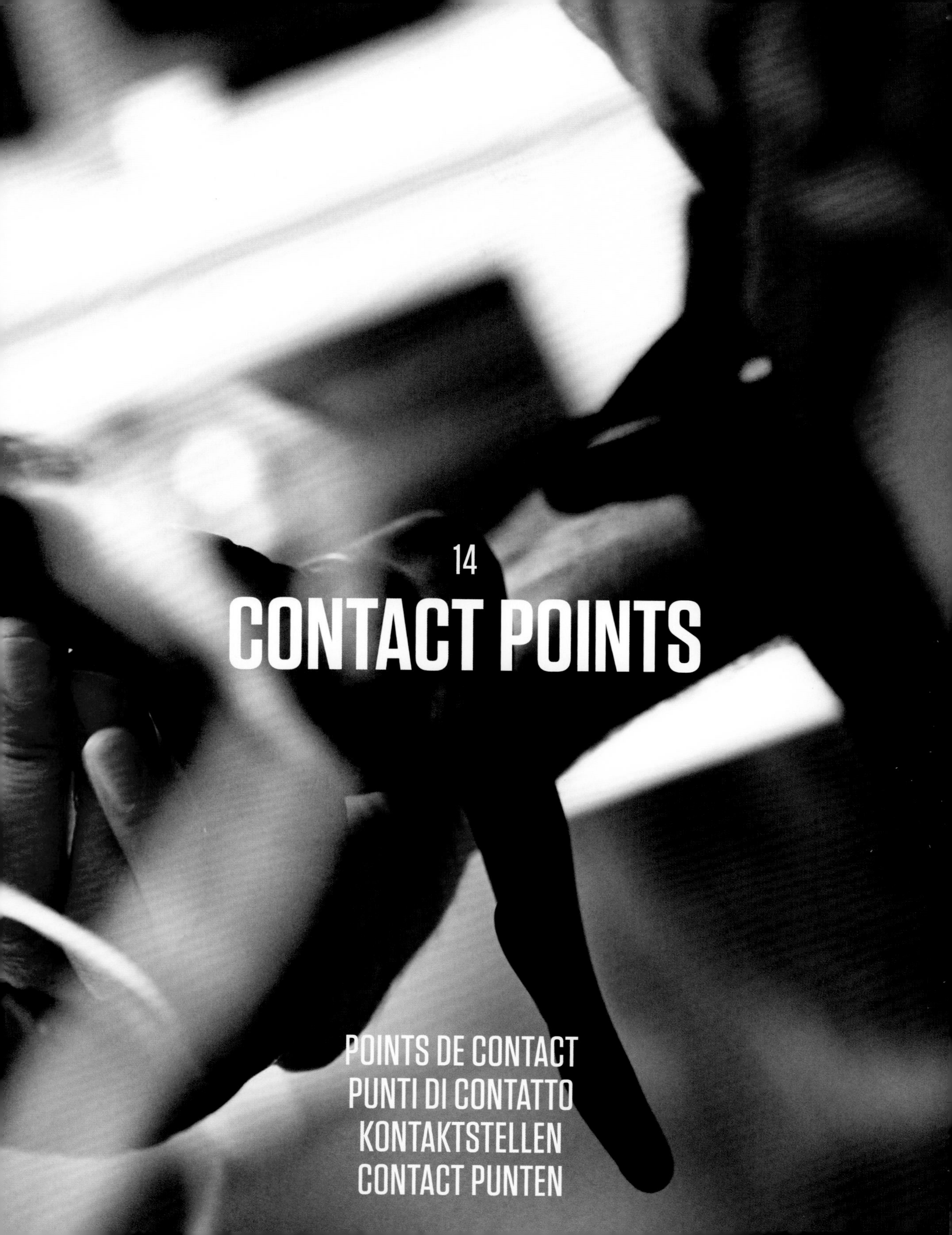

14
CONTACT POINTS

POINTS DE CONTACT
PUNTI DI CONTATTO
KONTAKTSTELLEN
CONTACT PUNTEN

Clean bar tape is the clear sign of a professional's bike

During a Grand Tour, putting fresh bar tape on bikes can be a bind, what with 20 or so machines to do. So it's a job usually done in rotation, and not after every stage. Individual riders can be pretty fastidious and demanding, so may demand more regular freshen ups.

Whenever I see freshly fitted white bar tape, I am reminded of a passage from *The Rider* by Tim Krabbé:

"Kleber is standing in front of me. We greet each other. I point to his bars. 'New tape?' He smiles apologetically. 'For morale.'"

Exactly. Fresh bar tape indicates a state of mind—as, for that matter, does a spotlessly clean bike. It's important to racers as well as mechanics. Former world pursuit champion and Six Day star Tony Doyle would agonise over the wrap of his bars and have them redone, even minutes before a pursuit match, if they weren't perfect. Nothing left to chance, pride in your workplace, as it were. And team mechanics are a particularly proud bunch. All bikes need to look like new on the start line and there is little to rival the look of pristine white bar tape.

As road surfaces became harder, forks more rigid, tyres narrower and harder, cushioned bar tape became an almost inevitable development. Ambrosio bike ribbon, which emerged in the early '80s, was a revelation. With a lightly textured surface and a subtle cambered cross-section, when applied the tape left you with a smooth, comfortable surface which was washable.

It was a real step forward but more innovation was around the corner. Few were better placed to drive it than legendary handlebar, stem and bicycle maker Cinelli. In 1987, the first version of their now legendary cork tape was produced, which has spawned countless (generally inferior) imitations ever since. Cinelli's cork tape was in fact blended with polyurethane to give a perfect bar covering, being lightweight as well as shock and sweat absorbent.

A seemingly incongruous part of the bicycle, handlebar tape has become as much a fashion statement as a functional product. Every bike can be personalised and have its look fine tuned by judicious bar tape choice. Who can forget the striking celeste bar tape used on the early Bianchi bikes, or the white cotton on Saronni's wine red Mexico? There was Claudio Chiappucci's denim-coloured cork on those beautiful Carrera bikes; the distinctive amber Benotto seen on ANC's Peugeots; the red, white and blue Bastille Day tape that featured on the Super U Raleigh team bikes of Fignon and co. in the 1989 Tour. Other notables are the quirky white plastic tape seen on several Spanish team bikes, including the Giants of Once and the Pinarellos of Banesto not too long ago. This tape really did fly in the face of logic as it was hard, rough and slippery when wet, but it can be clearly seen on several teams' bikes if you look hard enough. It's easy to fit and undoubtedly low in cost, which may be why several team mechanics favour it even though it looks like it's come off the handle of a cheap supermarket-bought tennis racket.

There is so much available that choosing a type of tape now is no easy task, let alone choosing the colour. But I can help you there, if you want to keep it classy: fit white. Always white.

Handlebar choice and set up

Along with stems and sometimes forks, handlebars should be changed after a bad crash. Scuffed bar tape from a crash should be removed and replaced and the bars inspected before retaping them. If there is any damage to the bar, no matter how slight, then replace it.

T hirty or so years ago, choice in quality handlebars was pretty limited. Cinelli, the number one manufacturer at the time, kept things pretty simple. If you were a big guy you rode Merckx pattern Model 66. If you were a little shorter in stature then the Giro d'Italia 64 pattern bars would be more suitable. For many, though, the 'Crit' model 65 was a favourite. This was despite a very restricted hand position on the tops: the bars swept away from the stem almost immediately leaving little space. Their popularity is explained by the drops, where the upper profile avoided your forearm when sprinting.

Choose one of those three, pick a width (generally by holding a pair in the local shop with your arms parallel) and you were done. Tighten your levers up—after getting them level by sitting the bars on a flat surface—and your ergonomic consideration was exhausted.

Sure there were other brands to choose from but most firms offered the same designs as their competitors. The introduction of anatomic bars shook things up a bit, and they were adopted by some looking for comfort.

Measurements are carefully checked on each rider's bike to make sure that their bike fit details are adhered to. Each mechanic has his own method of setting up the bikes in his charge. Handlebar profiles are generally chosen by the rider and the shape they choose will dictate to some degree exactly where their levers can go.

In the 1990s anatomic bars were all the rage—even though they were anything but. In recent years, however, the new compact-style bars have become very popular for good reason. Everybody could benefit from analysing their current handlebar setup once in a while. There is no point having a bike with drop handlebars and then saying you never use the drops or you can't reach the brake levers. In many cases we make do with what we have but with a little effort and moderate investment you can often improve the ergonomics of your bike and end up with a comfortable, more efficient and better handling bike than you ever thought possible.

Rectifying these issues can be one of the most liberating things you can do, as often someone's inability to descend or corner well comes down to bad bar set up.

The pro peloton has always been a place where tradition prevails but recently their collective minds have taken a more scientific approach. Riders have now started using narrow width bars to gain an aerodynamic advantage and 'slamming' the stem down as low as possible, which isn't always the best ergonomic approach, but so much is placed on being aero. Mechanics will sometimes add extra padding to the top of the bar if the rider needs to get aero, but still wants some comfort and height on the tops. Riders have also started to opt for shallow drop bars, for comfort reasons and because, for the sprinters out there, they are stiffer.

The clips that fasten the brake levers to the handlebars need some special care. Use a grip paste to ensure a secure footing and prevent damage to carbon bars

Loosening the clips on the levers to slot them over the handlebars sometimes needs them to be removed completely, getting them back on again is a fiddle

Omega Pharma—Quick-Step team mechanic Dominique Landuyt has his own special tool to set the height of the brake levers. When building several bikes quickly and identically this type of reference tool is essential.

The levers should be absolutely level, this takes time and a spirit level. A test ride before taping the bars will save a lot of time, because once it's on adjusting the lever height isn't recommended.

Brake and gear cables need to be secured firmly to the handlebars before the taping process can commence. Electrical tape is the best way to do this (see the image on page 236).

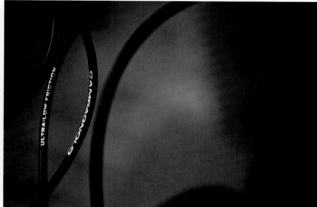

Nearly every modern stem type has a removable faceplate with two or four bolts in most cases. It is very important to ensure that the faceplate is parallel otherwise uneven forces may be applied to your handlebar's clamp area. The bolts should be tightened gradually and evenly and in the case of a four-bolt-design in an alternate zigzag pattern much like a cylinder head on an engine. A torque wrench is invaluable in this area to ensure you don't write off your bars fitting them!

How to wrap a bar

BEFORE YOU START

Brake lever hoods can be fragile, especially if they're getting on a bit, so take it easy when pulling them clear of the taping area.

Wrap the bar-tops with electrical tape, this neatens up the cables and also protects the bar from sweat damage

Add an extra layer of tape for riding the rough stuff, or use plumbing lagging on the tops, it makes a massive difference over cobblestones and on cyclo-cross bikes, especially if you suffer hand pain or nerve pinching.

Make sure you have all the tools and material you need close to hand, once you've started wrapping you don't need to be reaching across the room for a pair of scissors.

A Start with a small overlap at the open end of the bar of between 5mm and 10mm, depending on the thickness and flexibility of the tape. Too little and your end plug will never stay put; too much and you will never get the end plug in. Start inboard and wind in an anti-clockwise direction as you face the front of the bike (i.e. the right hand side of the bike is on your left hand side).

B Wind up the tape, keeping an even tension and firm hold as you work up the bar. Take note of the tape profile. If you wrap the tape with too much overlap it will be lumpy and you will run out. If you wind with too little overlap it will also get lumpy and you will almost certainly have a bit of handlebar peeping through by the time you get to the radius of the bend.

C If you fit the brake lever clip cover strip, be careful not to let it fall off—otherwise you may find it stuck to the carpet or sole of your shoe by the time you reach the lever body. Better to stick it somewhere convenient until you get to this point.

D The transition round the lever is one of the most difficult to complete successfully. If you haven't put your brake lever clip strip in place, now is the time to do it. Maintain the tension and the angle of the tape as it passes behind the lever. This can be a real test of dexterity. Plan where the tape will meet the lever. Campagnolo users in particular must take care here as a wayward bit of tape can foul the mechanism causing the gears to malfunction.

E The body of the lever and the clip should now be completely covered. The trick here is not to do things too slowly. Keep the tension even and regain the same spacing as your previous overlap. You are ready to finish off the job but to do so well it is essential to maintain a consistent winding angle. Do not try to straighten up immediately, maintain the tension to achieve the perfect finish.

F With a sharp pair of scissors cut the tape away at an angle, in effect mitring it, to leave you with a nice crisp edge to terminate.

G Most tape comes with its own finishing strips but they will either peel off or let go of the tape when you least need it. A really neat method is to superglue the mitred end, but this is not always possible as some current tapes will not stay glued up.

H The orientation of your finishing plug should be carefully noted before pushing fully home. Some plugs are plain, so this is not important, but if the plug carries an image or logo you may drop a point here for sloppy workmanship. And there you have it—well, almost. You still have the other side to do.

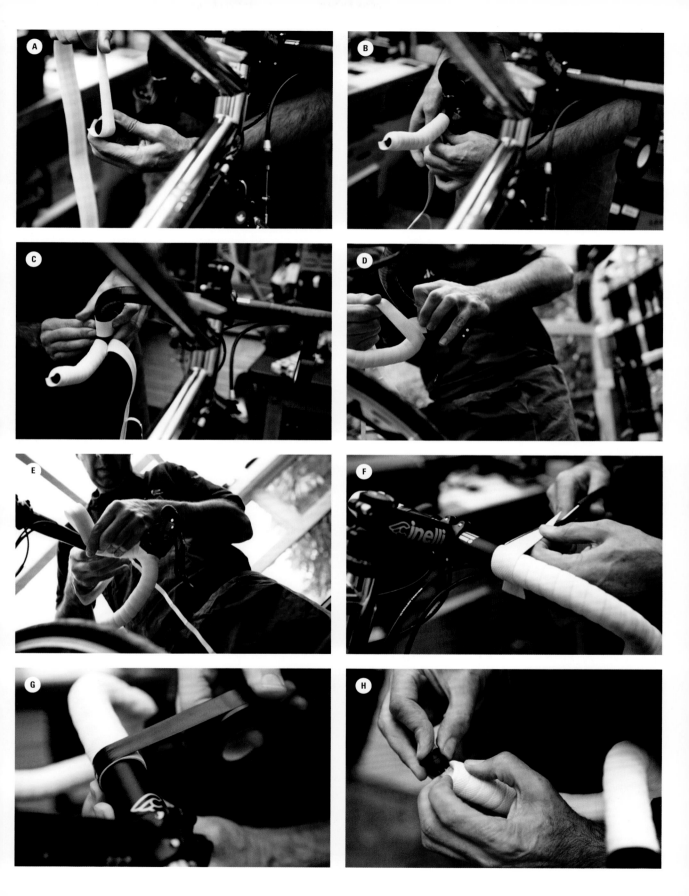

Cleats and pedals

Often neglected — out of sight, out of mind — your pedal and shoe set up should be examined regularly if injury is to be avoided and efficiency maximised. After all, this could be regarded as the most critical contact point on the bike. The right choice of interface between rider and his or her machine is the foundation of a good bike-fit and not something to be taken lightly. Regardless of the pedal system you use it is important to monitor cleat and pedal condition as the gradual erosion of both elements can reduce efficiency at best and at worst become a serious safety issue.

For many years, riders used metal clips and straps to secure their feet, adding a slotted cleat to the bottom of their shoes to prevent any unwanted slippage. All very well but exact cleat position was imperative and nailing cleats to the soles of your shoes in precisely the right place was a bit of a lottery.

Most readers of this book will have embraced the clipless pedal. The exception will be those with biomechanical issues which mean lateral movement for release is not an option, the track racing *cognoscenti*, and a few luddites. It was back in 1984 that French ski manufacturer Look applied their 'quick release' technology to the bicycle pedal in 1984, and I think it is safe to say they still dominate the market today, with Shimano a close second. They each offer excellent performance, though with their metal reinforced pedal bodies, Shimano's current SPD SL models offer the greatest durability.

Since both systems rely on the nose of the plastic cleat to retain your foot, this section wears through repetitive stopping and starting, not to mention all that waddling around the local coffee shop. In turn, the security of your shoe to pedal interface will deteriorate. If left too long the cleat can and will eventually fail suddenly with potentially dire consequences. For that reason it is important to check the integrity of the pedal body and the cleat and ditch any worn component before it's too late.

Other systems such as Speedplay turn the whole concept of cleat and pedal on its head. Whilst the hard alloy material selected for their cleat wears very well, it is vitally important to keep the moving parts clean and lubricated to ensure reliable entry and release.

Bearing health on all pedals should be checked regularly and any play that may have developed assessed. A tiny bit of movement between axle and pedal body is normal even straight out the box but too much is a sure-fire sign that the bearings are on their way out. It is also worth remembering that pedals with worn bodies or bearings can track unevenly, eventually resulting in injury. Knee and ankle joints are particularly vulnerable, so take care.

Today's almost ubiquitous clipless pedal systems are, for the most part, tolerant to slight cleat positional error.

In an ideal world your foot should be firmly retained in its optimum position yet given some element of freedom to move while held securely. In the event of a fall you need the system to set you free.

If your foot is held against its will as it moves though the entire pedal stroke, your knees will often be the first part of your body to complain. If these warning signs are ignored then serous injury can occur.

Once in a while you should take a good look at the condition of your pedals and cleats. A few minutes spent on this task will make entry and exit smoother and your ride creak free. Lightly lube the pivot pins of the pedals and the spring to keep everything moving freely.

Clean the pedal body and check for excessive wear of the top plate and bearings. A quick squirt of a silicone-based spray or furniture polish on the cleat will also help ease release and entry. Never use grease or spray lube as it will attract dirt.

Creaks on modern bikes can often be tracked to the pedal crank interface. Titanium axles are notorious for this so if you are the wrong side of 75kg you might want to consider turning a blind eye to a few extra grams and opt instead for a steel axle variant of your pedal of choice. Always grease the pedal threads prior to installation and use a copper slip compound on titanium axles.

Make sure you use a pedal washer if the crank and pedal manufacture dictate this, and check the installation instructions carefully before fitting one.

Many modern pedal designs no longer feature 15mm spanner flats on the axle, relying instead on an Allen key to fit them to the crank. Recent generations of pedal are lighter than their predecessors but in general more difficult to remove.

If you are happy with your cleat position make sure you record it before you remove the worn one for replacement. A gold paint marker pen is perfect for tracing the position on a black sole.

Make sure you add a dab of grease or anti-seize compound to the threads of the bolts or inserts. The bottom of your shoes are exposed to the elements and seized fittings are bad news.

Once you have prepped your shoe you can get on with fitting the new cleat. To prevent unwanted movement on stiff carbon-soled shoes, manufacturers often provide a gritty patch to reduce the chance of unwanted slippage. I normally add a smear of Finish Line Fiber Grip between the two surfaces to make sure that the cleat does not slide around and to reduce the amount of tightening force you need to use. After your first shakedown ride you should nip everything up to make sure it stays put.

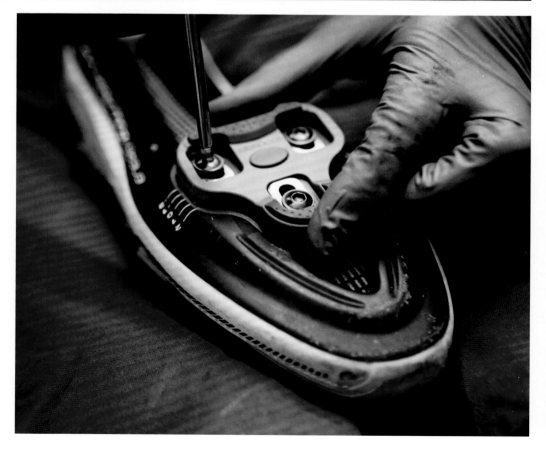

The last remaining handmade part of the modern bicycle

The human derrière has altered little during our evolution and yet saddle manufacturers keep coming up with new ideas about this, perhaps the most sensitive of contact points. For years the trusty leather saddle with its hide upper stretched over a sprung steel frame sufficed, but the nature of this type of saddle required a sometimes lengthy breaking in period as it conformed to your shape and was ultimately prone to environmental conditions. Neglect a seasoned saddle at your peril, leather needs to be maintained if it is to remain durable and compliant so a ritual of 'feeding' with a suitable conditioner was required. Add to this scenario the fact that this type of saddle was generally pretty heavy and you can see why the performance road market was hungry for alternative ways to regulate the distance form your posterior to the pedals.

Many riders who constantly chop and change saddles looking for posterior utopia would actually be better off seeking out an experienced bike fitter. Nowadays many retailers in the high street offer you the opportunity to try before you buy and can advise on suitability for pelvic dimension if nothing else.

The bottom line is that your sit bones will help you choose, so it is worth taking a little time to experiment; although this can become costly so seeking the advice of an experienced retailer is a wise move. Gel pads and cut-outs may help relieve undesirable pressure and titanium rails might help dissipate a small amount of road buzz. But even if you get part of the way towards day-long comfort in the saddle often the root cause of any discomfort is actually a poor position on the bike... which is another can of worms altogether.

Something that rarely gets mentioned in component choice these days is comfort. It's as if it's bad for racers, a thing only for commuters or not-so-serious riders. But since bike fit is now an industry in itself, I wonder what has happened to the saddle, the bit that really connects us to our bikes. Has rider physiology really changed that much? Does today's average rider now differ so much from someone who rode, say, 20 or 30 years ago?

Getting a professional cyclist to change his saddle is a bit like asking a pro golfer to change putter. Even so, when fitting a new saddle, most will probably only consider how it looks on the bike before considering how it fits their bum — because, let's face it, svelte saddles look fast. The only way to know whether a different saddle will suit you better is to try it, which isn't always possible.

The 1980s was the seminal development decade for the racing bike saddle. Italian models dominated the professional peloton with the likes of the Turbo, Turbomatic, Rolls, Regal and Concor. The leather saddle was wiped out as quickly as toe clips and straps were once Look introduced clipless pedals. Pros demanded a saddle that was comfortable from the moment you sat on it. No longer could they spend training hours breaking in new saddles and waste resting hours washing and waxing their mounts. The plastic moulded saddle ensured a predictable fit from the off; the main problem was finding the one that suited you best. The new leather — or suede-covered, plastic-based saddles by the likes of San Marco, Selle Italia and Cinelli ruled the peloton.

The main technical problem that seemed to mar the '80s saddle was the low sides that covered the rails. These flaps would snag on the seatpost cradle, creaking and rubbing annoyingly. This even caused problems on Selle Italia's first foray into lightweight

After three weeks in the saddle Grand Tour riders succumb to saddle sores, boils and much worse.

Laurent Fignon suffered such an affliction that he said contributed to him losing the 1989 Tour de France.

Mechanics have been known to swap saddles, add extra cushioning, and even cut chunks out of a saddle to relieve the pressure on a problem area. Lightweight saddles are less popular with the bigger riders, the rouleurs and track specialists who spend a lot of time seated. They may opt for a stronger, more substantial yet heavier saddle with more padding that helps soak up the road shock.

Always check for sharp edges in your seat tube before inserting your seatpost. In the case of carbon seatposts, scratches are potentially structurally damaging. Don't forget to coat the section of the post that enters the frame with a suitable assembly paste.

Carefully follow the manufacturer's instructions when installing your saddle. Carbon saddle rails in particular need careful handling, and other new lightweight alloys often have clamp zones that should not be ignored.

Personal preference often prevails when it comes to precise saddle alignment. A spirit level is a good place to start.

Saddle height setup. Most commonly measured from the centre of the bottom bracket to the top of the saddle following the line of the seat tube.

Most riders have a saddle 'out of the box' but there are a few riders who have a persona specification or a non-sponsored saddle.

saddles, the titanium railed Flite. The solution was to cut away the sides, which made sense to a point, but as an exposed seatpost cradle isn't always perfectly smooth it can cause all sorts of bother to your inner thighs, especially if you are a few kilos heavier than your average Spanish climber. The chafing can be murder.

Physiological studies and computer analysis has opened up a science that has revolutionised the process of fitting you to a bike, but the saddles we now sit on and the shoes we now wear are harder and stiffer than a cricket bat. Have we evolved gel pouches in our buttocks? Have the cobbles of Flanders and Roubaix joined together a little more? Or perhaps there's some kind of weird machismo in the desire to sit on a brick?

This recent trend for ever-lighter saddles has become ridiculous. Even if a pair of shorts now has a decent pad, a saddle needs to have an ability to soak up road shock and keep you connected to the bike. Many old pros say it's better to sit than stand. Sitting on the bike when riding fast, especially over rough ground, keeps you connected to the bike, which keeps the bike going in a straight line. And the longer you can sit down in comfort, the further you will go, and the faster. The debate surrounding the width of the saddle matching the width of your sit bones is wearing a little thin. Most riders know an over-soft and squishy saddle can be just as painful as a very hard one, no matter how well positioned the sit bones are. It's all about the support underneath, and it's a fact that thin, over-hard saddles wear you out quicker.

Another long running debate is hole-in-the-saddle or no hole. Recent designs from brands like Fizik use central, pressure-relieving channels which may satisfy both camps but, as with everything to do with saddles, some experimentation will be required.

Just because you blew a heap of your hard-earned cash on a new saddle does not mean it will last indefinitely. Shell sag and upper

padding deterioration varies — some models are more prone to it than others. It is worth noting any surface undulations when you buy your saddle and comparing your weathered saddle with a new version at the very least once a season. That way you can easily monitor any change. This is important as excessive sag or compression will actually alter your saddle height.

Other than that it is pretty obvious that an occasional wash is hygienic and a good idea. Leather saddles benefit from the use of suitable cleaners and treatments that can be sourced from the automotive industry. Using these will preserve your investment. Synthetics are happy with some lukewarm (not hot) water and a mild detergent that does not contain alkaline.

Don't neglect the underside of your saddle. During the winter months when many of you still insist on riding without mudguards, it can become a pretty grim place. The accumulation of road detritus can also seize up any seatpost fittings, so keep it clean under there.

15

CLEANING AND LUBRICATION

NETTOYAGE ET LUBRIFICATION
PULIZIA E LUBRIFICAZIONE
REINIGUNG UND LUBRICATION
REINIGEN EN SMEREN

Professional riders can be fined for a dirty bike...

Dozens of cleaning products are commonly available and each mech I know has their favourites but consider the following as a basic checklist: A mild frame and component wash. Avoid car shampoo as it can leave waxy residue on brake pads and rims. Resist the temptation to use washing up liquid as it can contain alkalis and salt that will eventually attack certain finishes. A powerful degreaser — but be judicious in where you use it. A water displacing lubricant. Ideal for applying to all pivot points, especially after washing or a particularly wet ride.

Roll up to the start of a race or a training camp with a dirty bike and expect a fine. This was once one of the rules of the professional bike racing world, back when riders usually had only two bikes and had to look after themselves between races. These days riders often have four or five spare bikes, so one is usually always in pristine condition. Any pro mechanic will tell you that today's professional riders are hopeless at bike washing. Getting closer to your bike will mean you spot problems before they turn into failures. Dismantling and cleaning off everything allows you to inspect the components' condition very quickly. This is one significant plus of owning a clean and well maintained bike.

But the simple fact is that neglecting your cleaning and maintenance duties will shorten your bike's life and compromise its performance sooner or later. It's as simple as that.

The first thing you should invest in is a workstand that will hold the bike securely at a comfortable level. There are many types on the market but Park Tool make some excellent products, including the PRS25. This stand is lightweight and portable which means it is easy to manoeuvre and tuck away somewhere when not in use.

When I am faced with a particularly filthy bike a basic clean up is essential before an assessment of service work required can be carried out. Initially I spray the bike with a frame cleaning agent such as ProGold bike wash, taking care to avoid all the bearings. It is wise to set your stall out before you start so you can work quickly, because even the mildest cleaners should not be left to act too long.

You should have plenty of clean water in a bucket and a couple of sponges, or even a hose with an adjustable spray head. This will allow you to use more force on things like rims and tyres and reduce to a trickle to rinse the paintwork. A few microfiber cloths for drying duties are not a bad idea either.

Once most of the surface dirt is removed you can decide what other cleaning is required and attend to it in more detail. Cleaning the bike will allow closer inspection of things like rim or tyre damage, brake pad condition and may even help detect a crack in the frame during the drying off process.

I prefer to remove chains to clean them and in most cases use a quick link from someone like KMC to make this easier. Where such a tool is unavailable or using it undesirable, the chain can be blasted with an aerosol cleaner on to an old towel. This will flush out a significant amount of dirt.

Chainrings are easily cleaned and, provided they are not too dirty, can be left on the cranks. If they are really filthy remove them but pay close attention to the orientation before removal — this will avoid mistakes when you reinstall them.

Cassettes should always be removed for cleaning to avoid the ingress of any cleaning agent into your hub bearings. As long as you are methodical and observe the splines on the freehub and sprockets, everything should go back together without a hitch. If in doubt lay each component out sequentially and take a picture.

So not then just an exercise in vanity. Bike cleaning should be something that you regularly undertake to preserve your pride and joy. It will make your cycling experience safer and more enjoyable, which can't be bad, can it?

This parts washer from RoZone works without the help of nasty solvents, relying on environmentally friendly Bio Remediation technology.

This is not strictly a must have for the average home mechanic, but it saves a professional time and money. The washer's microscopic bacteria eat the oil deposits and leave even the most grimy parts sparkling. The liquid is pumped through a brush head as you agitate the dirt. I don't know where I'd be without mine.

A filthy chain contaminates every single thing it comes into contact with. If you're fitting a new chain, make sure you clean everything else that touched it, including your chainrings.

Chainrings should be removed to carry out efficient cleaning. Cranks also benefit from a bit of a bath while you have the opportunity. Just avoid getting cleaning agents near bearings.

Brake callipers have a tough life. Because they are mounted over the tyres they get a lot of weather chucked at them, and the result is that the pivots tend to gradually seize up without you noticing. A good scrub and lube every so often is not a bad idea. This is also a perfect time to check pad wear and replace if necessary.

Old water bottles make perfect containers for solvents and cleaning fluids, not least because they can be stored in your bottle cage when you are cleaning your bike.

It's all very well stripping every trace of lubricant off a part during cleaning but it's important to use a quality lubricant on all the pivots once you're finished.

Your transmission will need the most regular attention of any part of your bike. Lubrication should be carried out regularly but it is unwise to keep drowning the chain in oil. To maximise the life of your transmission regular degreasing will wash out any contaminants before adding the fresh lubricant of your choice. Busy schedule? Industrial strength Big Wipes are ready soaked in degreasing agent and make light work of a dirty chain. The secret to a perfectly maintained transmission is regular degreasing and removal of all traces of dirt.

After any cleaning operation you need to make sure that all pivot points are re-lubricated. Brake pivots and springs will need attention to ensure smooth operation.

Parallelogram derailleurs have four pivot pins. For optimum shifting performance, these must be kept lubricated and able to move freely with as little friction as possible.

During a strip down service I like to take the opportunity to get up close and personal with each frame I am working on. Firstly I clean off any dirt and then examine each tube looking for paint defects and potential cracks. Waxing the frame with a suitable polish can highlight frame defects. Cleaning and polishing should be seen as an exercise in safety rather than vanity.

Once you have cleaned and dried the chain you should apply a drop of your chosen lubricant to each roller in turn. Avoid the temptation to drown the chain. Little and often is the order of the day, wiping away any excess with a clean bit of rag.

COMPONENT AND RECOMMENDED LUBE

Chain: Progold / Finish Line dry / Finish Line / White Lightning
Hub bearings: Finish Line Teflon grease / Campagnolo LB100
Headset bearings: Finish Line Teflon grease / Campagnolo LB100
Bottom brackets: Finish Line Teflon grease / Campagnolo LB100
Cables: Shimano cable grease
Brake and derailleur pivots: Finish Line 1 step clean and lube

Campagnolo LB-100 grease for the most critical jobs and also for Ergopower lever rebuilds. I tend to use Finish Line Teflon fortified grease for everyday lubrication and assembly duties and the third lubricant that I use in my workshop is a heavy duty blue grease that comes from Exus. It is a bit too thick and draggy for high performance roles but in extreme conditions such as winter bike hubs and headsets etc. it works really well… During the summer, light wax lubes are sufficient, but when conditions worsen a heavier weight wet lube is a better option.

In the upper image we can see the torque wrench in its pre-set 'drive position' and immediately after it has clicked, warning us that the desired torque setting has been reached. The setting is dialled in before use.

It is a measuring device so it's important to hold the torque wrench correctly if you want to be sure that you are applying an accurate amount of force to the fastener in question.

Effetto Mariposa and Norbar produce excellent quality torque wrenches. It is quite common to have two wrenches in your toolkit: one for the heavy stuff like bottom bracket cups and cranks and the other for low torque tasks such as handlebars, stems and seatposts.

How tight is tight?

Almost every sensitive bicycle component will have a maximum bolt torque setting printed on it somewhere. If not there will certainly be reference made to it on the manufacturer's website or in any instruction manual that accompanies the product.

New materials and creative designs that pare structures down to the absolute minimum to reduce weight bring added responsibility to mechanic and end user. As such any torque recommendations should be strictly adhered to if you want to avoid malfunction at best and catastrophic failure at worst.

What follows is a guide to some of the most popular components on a modern racing bicycle and their stipulated torque settings. Handlebars, stems and seatposts will all benefit from the application of specific assembly paste to increase the friction generated without resorting to using more torque than the manufacturer recommends.

COMPONENT	TORQUE IN NEWTON METRES
Pedals into crank	30–35Nm
Chainring fixing bolts (steel)	9Nm
Chainring fixing bolts (alloy)	5Nm
Square taper-fitting crank arm bolts	35–44Nm
Track axle nuts to frame (fixed wheel bike wheel nuts)	25Nm front wheel and 35Nm rear wheel
Hub cone lock nuts	15Nm
Brake levers to handlebars	6–8Nm
Aheadstem binder bolts	11Nm single bolt and 9Nm double bolts
Quick release lever (closing of lever)	9–12Nm
Seatpost fixing bolt	30Nm
Sealed bottom bracket cartridge (square taper or Octalink)	50–70Nm
Shoe pedal cleat bolts (not Speedplay)	8Nm

SOME MANUFACTURERS' SPECIFIC RECOMMENDATIONS

Deda Zero 100 Handlebar stem—face plate and steerer bolts	8Nm
Deda Zero 1 stem	8Nm
Ritchey WCS Handlebar stem	5Nm
3t ARX Pro stem	5Nm
Campagnolo Ultra-Torque bottom bracket cups	35Nm
Campagnolo Ultra-Torque crank bolt	42–60Nm
Campagnolo Cassette lockring	40Nm for 11v or 50Nm for 10v
Shimano Hollowtech II bottom bracket cups	35–50Nm
Shimano Hollowtech II bearing adjustment cap	0.7–1.5Nm
Shimano Cassette lockring	35–50Nm
SRAM Red Chainset crank bolts	12–15Nm
SRAM Mega-Exo bottom bracket cups	34–41Nm
Colnago C59 Seatpost clamp	6Nm
Pinarello Dogma seat clamp	3Nm

This list is just a guide. Please refer to manufacturers' recommendations for exact details

Biographies

GUY ANDREWS is the founding editor of Rouleur magazine, which he started in 2006. Before then he worked as a freelance writer and editor and before that as a bike mechanic, teacher and an enthusiastic, but not particularly successful, bike racer. He has also written several books on the subject of fixing bicycles and bicycle technology, notably The Custom Road Bike (Laurence King) and Road Bike Maintenance (Bloomsbury) and has edited all of Rouleur's highly regarded photography annuals and books.
www.rouleur.cc

ROHAN DUBASH has been a cyclist since 1979. His love of the machinery, the etiquette and the sport itself led him to enter the cycling industry in 1981. Since then Rohan has worked for several high end bicycle emporiums and also contributed technical articles to publications including Cycling Weekly and Rouleur magazine. He now works as a freelance bicycle consultant, fitter and mechanic.
www.doctord.co.uk

TAZ DARLING is often found shooting the world's biggest bike races, although she's keen to state that she isn't a cycling photographer per se. Her reportage work has featured in Red Bulletin, Vice and Embrocation magazines. Taz has also worked for Rouleur books as both a picture editor, most notably on critically acclaimed books Coppi and Maglia Rosa, and as a regular contributor to Rouleur photography annuals.
www.tazdarling.com

Suppliers

Chris Snook for Finish Line lubricants,
Wheels Manufacturing bearing tools,
Park frame and workshop tools and
Shimano components
www.madison.co.uk

Sealey tools for workbench and tool storage
www.sealey.co.uk

Julian Candy for Beta Allen keys and pliers
www.primetools.co.uk

Chris King for Aheadsets, tools and spares
www.chrisking.com

Mark at Evolution
www.evolutionimports.co.uk

Tom Marchment for Cyclus tools
www.i-ride.co.uk

Rory Hitchens for Effetto Mariposa
Lezyne tools
www.upgradebikes.co.uk

Bryan for Kestrel workstand and wheel rack
www.kestrelcyclestands.co.uk

David Rollason for Norbar torque wrenches
www.norbar.com

Robin Lewis for Rozone Parts Washer
www.rozone.co.uk

Andrew for VAR frame tools
JD Whiskers 01438 798 772

Valeria Cavallo for Cinelli Xcr frame
www.cinelli.it

Claudia Vianino for Vittoria tyres
www.vittoria.com

Tom Gray for Zefal HPX frame pumps
www.zyro.co.uk

Simon Beatson for Silca track pumps
and Challenge tubular tyres
www.paligap.cc

Shelly Childs for Continental tyres
www.cambriantyres.co.uk

Kerstin for P&K Lie truing stand and spoke key
www.pklie.de

Joshua Riddle for Campagnolo components
www.campagnolo.com

Geraldine Bergenon for SRAM components
www.sram.com

Mosquito Bikes
www.mosquito-bikes.co.uk

Cyclefit
www.cyclefit.co.uk

Ian Whittingham and Jason Turner
from Sigma Sport
www.sigmasport.co.uk

Grant Young from Condor Cycles
www.condorcycles.com

We were very lucky to
have had the help of
Zoe Wassall from Great
Northern Locations.
www.greatnorthern
locations.co.uk

We are also indebted
to the incredibly
helpful prop building
team of Cathal and
Laszlo MacIlwaine.

Also, huge thanks to
all the mechanics who
allowed us to point
our cameras into their
trucks or who have
helped in some way
with this book—Derek
Mclay, Harry Rowland,
Frèdèric Bassey
and all the guys at
Mavic, Alberto Masi,
Steve Snowling,
Dominique Landuyt,
Kris Withington,
Yoshiaki Nagasawa,
Roger Theel and
Rune Kristiansen.

Thanks

Guy Andrews would like to thank: All the team's staff for their patience, notably Alessandro Tegner from OPQS, Ben Coates from Trek and Tim Vanderjeugd from Leopard Trek (now with Orica GreenEDGE). Also Elisa Madiot at FDJ, Hendrik Redant at United Healthcare, Malte Stampe, Veronica Passoni and everybody at Vittoria and Michel Lethernet and all of the support team at Mavic. Everybody at Rouleur, especially Rob Johnston who designed this book and put up with edit after edit... And lastly to Nick Ashcroft and Charlotte Croft at Bloomsbury for all their patience and hard work to make it happen.

Rohan Dubash would like to thank: Mum and Dad for putting up with all the bikes in our house and my Brother for getting me to fix his bikes. Kevin Jones and Keith Bentley for introducing me to cycling and the saying "Campag throughout." Tony Butterworth for nurturing my love of Italian bikes and Pete Spowage for taking me under his wing at my first cycling club.

Taz Darling would like to thank: Ned and Essie for keeping me so grounded. To Gus Wylie who made his passion for highly sophisticated colour and space truly infectious and taught me to know when I was really working. To the team at Rouleur for being brave enough to trust the off-beat and for producing such a beautiful showcase for our work. To Edwin Ingram for always finding the last 5 per cent that nobody else can. Finally to everyone who graciously allows me access to their everyday lives with my camera.

"I have a unique way of looking at bicycles. A good bicycle and its components are beautiful things to me. I'm not just talking about the appearance, but also how the frame and components show the dreams of those who made them."

GIANNI BUGNO